# Beginning Swift Games Development for iOS

## Develop 2D and 3D games Using Apple's SceneKit and SpriteKit

### Second Edition

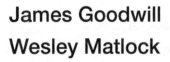

James Goodwill

Wesley Matlock

Apress®

*Beginning Swift Games Development for iOS: Develop 2D and 3D games Using Apple's SceneKit and SpriteKit*

James Goodwill
Highlands Ranch, Colorado, USA

Wesley Matlock
Kansas City, Missouri, USA

ISBN-13 (pbk): 978-1-4842-2309-3
DOI 10.1007/978-1-4842-2310-9

ISBN-13 (electronic): 978-1-4842-2310-9

Library of Congress Control Number: 2017942793

Managing Director: Welmoed Spahr
Editorial Director: Todd Green
Acquisitions Editor: Aaron Black
Development Editor: James Markham
Technical Reviewer: Bruce Wade
Coordinating Editor: Jessica Vakili

Distributed to the book trade worldwide by Springer Science+Business Media New York, 233 Spring Street, 6th Floor, New York, NY 10013. Phone 1-800-SPRINGER, fax (201) 348-4505, e-mail orders-ny@springer-sbm.com, or visit www.springeronline.com. Apress Media, LLC is a California LLC and the sole member (owner) is Springer Science + Business Media Finance Inc (SSBM Finance Inc). SSBM Finance Inc is a Delaware corporation.

For information on translations, please e-mail rights@apress.com, or visit www.apress.com.

Apress and friends of ED books may be purchased in bulk for academic, corporate, or promotional use. eBook versions and licenses are also available for most titles. For more information, reference our Special Bulk Sales–eBook Licensing web page at www.apress.com/bulk-sales.

Any source code or other supplementary material referenced by the author in this text is available to readers at www.apress.com/978-1-4842-2309-3. For detailed information about how to locate your book's source code, go to www.apress.com/source-code/.

Printed on acid-free paper

*To Christy Goodwill,*

*my awesome wife, you have supported me all of these years.*
*I could not have done a fraction of what I have without you. I love you.*

*Wesley Matlock - for Amy*

# Contents at a Glance

# Contents

# About the Authors

**James Goodwill** is a ten-time published author of books about leading technologies such as iOS, Swift, Objective C, Grails, Groovy, Java Servlets, JavaServer Pages (JSP), Tomcat, and Struts. He is a senior enterprise iOS and Java consultant in the Denver metro area and frequent speaker and article writer. You can find additional resources about Sprite Kit, Swift, and James himself at his blog at `www.jgoodwill.org`. You can also follow James on Twitter at `https://twitter.com/jamesgoodwill`.

**Wesley Matlock** is a professional independent iOS consultant in the Kansas City metro area. He has more than 20 years of development experience in several different platforms. He first started doing mobile development on the Compaq iPaq in the early 2000s. Today he enjoys developing on the iOS platform and bringing new ideas to life.

# About the Technical Reviewer

**Bruce Wade** is a software engineer from British Columbia, Canada. He started software development when he was 16 years old by coding his first website. He went on to study Computer Information Systems ad DeVry Institute of Technology in Calgary, then to further enhance his skills he studied Visual & Game Programming at The Art Institute Vancouver. Over the years he has worked for large corporations as well as several start-ups. His software experience has led him to utilize many different technologies including C/C++, Python, Objective-C, Swift, Postgres, and JavaScript. In 2012 he started the company Warply Designed to focus on mobile 2D/3D and OS X development. Aside from hacking out new ideas, he enjoys spending time hiking with his Boxer Rasco, working out, and exploring new adventures.

# Acknowledgments

This book could not have been written without the incredible folks at Apress. The idea of a Swift iOS gaming book began with a conversation with Steve Anglin and came to life with a great discussion about gaming and Apple with Michelle Lowman. Mark Powers and James Markham kept the book on the rails and brought it safely into the station. Bruce Wade made sure all of the technical statements made sense and the code compiled and ran successfully. I thank you all.

I want to send out a special thanks to Wes Matlock for taking over the Scene Kit section of the book when my father passed. I just did not have the time or energy to complete the second section of the book, and Wes stepped in without hesitation.

I also want to thank Deborah Saez for the wonderful artwork in the book. I highly recommend her. She is both very talented and a very hard worker. You can find her at www.deborahsaez.com/. Look her up.

Finally and most importantly, I want to thank the three girls in my life: Christy (my wonderful wife) and our daughters, Abby (who supplied a ton of inspiration) and Emma (who did a great technical review of the book). You three are the most important people in my life.

—James Goodwill

# Introduction

## Which Version of Swift Is Covered in This book?

This book covers version 3 of Swift and iOS version 10. As new versions are released, we will update the source for this book at both the Apress.com web site and James Goodwill's blog at www.jgoodwill.org.

## What This Book Is

Game apps are one of the most popular categories in the Apple iTunes App Store. Well, the introduction of the new Swift programming language will make game development even more appealing and easier to existing and future iOS app developers. In response, James Goodwill, Wesley Matlock, and Apress introduce you to this book, *Beginning Swift Games Development for iOS*.

In this book, you'll learn the fundamental elements of the new Swift language as applied to game development for iOS in 2D and 3D worlds using both Sprite Kit and Scene Kit, respectively.

## What You Need to Know

This book assumes you have a basic understanding of how to create applications for the iPhone using Xcode. You will also need a basic understanding of Apple's new programming language, Swift 3. We assume that you can download, install, and use the latest version of Xcode to create an application and run it on the iPhone simulator.

# What You Need to Have

In terms of hardware, you need an Intel-based Macintosh running Mountain Lion (OS X 10.8) or later. Regarding software, you need Xcode 8.x since that is the current version to include Swift 3. You can download Xcode from the App Store or Apple's developer web site at http://developer.apple.com.

# What's in This Book?

In Chapter 1, you'll learn about what Sprite Kit is and how you create a new Sprite Kit game using Xcode. You will then dive in and create the beginnings of a Sprite Kit game starting from scratch. You will learn about SKNodes and their subclasses, and you'll use an SKSpriteNode to add both a background node and a player node.

In Chapter 2, we will step back a bit and give you a deeper look at Sprite Kit scenes, including how scenes are built and why the order they are built in can change your game. The chapter will close with a discussion of Sprite Kit coordinate systems and anchor points as they relate to SKNodes.

In Chapter 3, you'll work with Sprite Kit's physics engine and collision detection. The chapter will begin with a discussion of SKPhysicsBody—the class used to simulate collision detection. You will then turn on gravity in the game world and see how that affects the nodes. After that, you will add a touch responder to propel the playerNode up into space, and finally you will learn how to handle node collisions.

In Chapter 4, you'll start adding some real functionality to your game. You'll begin by making some small changes to the current GameScene. After that, you will add additional orb nodes to collide into. You will then add scrolling to your scene, allowing you to make it look like the player is flying through space collecting orbs. Finally, you will start using the phone's accelerometer to move the player along the x-axis.

In Chapter 5, you'll refactor the orb node's layout one last time with the goal of enhancing playability. After that, you will learn how you can use SKActions to move an SKSpriteNode back and forth across the scene and then make that same node rotate forever. The chapter will close with a look at how you can add colorizing effects to an SKSpriteNode using a colorize action.

In Chapter 6, you'll see how to define particle emitters and how to leverage them in Sprite Kit games. After that, you will learn how you can use them to add engine exhaust to the playerNode whenever an impulse is applied to the physicsBody.

In Chapter 7, you'll see how you can use SKLabelNodes to add text to your Sprite Kit games. Specifically, you'll see how you how to add a label that keeps up with the number of impulses remaining for the spaceman to use, and then you'll see how you can add scoring to the game to keep up with the number of orbs the spaceman has collected.

In Chapter 8, you'll learn how to implement scene transitions using Sprite Kit's SKTransition class. You will look at some of the different types of built-in transitions Sprite Kit makes available to you. You will also see how you can control each scene during a transition. At the end of the chapter, you will take your newfound knowledge and add a menu scene to your SuperSpaceMan game.

In Chapter 9, you'll learn some Sprite Kit best practices; specifically, you will see how you can create your own subclasses of SKSpriteNode so that you can better reuse your nodes. You will then move on to changing your game to load all the sprites into a single texture atlas that you can reference when creating all future sprites. After that, you will move on to externalizing some of your game data so that designers and testers can change the game play. Finally, you will close out the chapter when you prune your node tree of all nodes that have fallen off the bottom of the screen.

In Chapter 10, you'll learn about what Scene Kit is and how to create a new Scene Kit game using Xcode. You will then dive in and create the beginnings of a Scene Kit game starting from scratch. You will learn to about SCNScene and SCNodes with a Scene Kit primer.

In Chapter 11, you'll learn more about the scene graph and some of the basics of Scene Kit. You will start to create your game by loading the spaceman from his Collada file. You will also learn about the Scene Kit primitive geometries by adding these as objects for the spaceman to avoid.

In Chapter 12, you'll learn how Scene Kit uses lighting and the type of lighting that is available to you in Scene Kit. You will also examine how materials are added onto the SCNNode, as well as how the camera is used within the scene.

In Chapter 13, you'll learn about the basics of animating the objects in your game. You will see a couple of different ways to animate the nodes to give you more than one way to do your animations. Once you have completed this chapter, all your objects will move within the scene.

In Chapter 14, you'll learn about collision detection within the scene. You will learn how to move the spaceman around the scene. Once you have the spaceman moving, you will learn how to detect when the spaceman runs into an obstacle.

In Chapter 15, you'll learn how to use a Sprite Kit scene within the Scene Kit scene. The chapter will show you how to create a screen to show you a timer that you will start when the user starts the game. The chapter will also show you how to display a "game over" screen and then restart the game.

In Chapter 16, you will learn the basics of the SceneKit Editor. This chapter will give you a basic understanding of creating a scene and various nodes visually in the editor. No coding will be done, but rather drag and dropping nodes and using the various editors to manipulate the objects.

# Part I

# Introduction to Spritekit

## Swift and Sprite Kit

In this part of this book, we will cover the basics of Sprite Kit including how you render and animate sprites, add physics and collision detection, and control your game play with the accelerometer. You will also look at how you add particle emitters to enhance the appearance of your game. We will cover everything you need to know to create your own Sprite Kit game.

# Setting Up Your Game Scene and Adding Your First Sprites

SpriteKit is Apple's exciting 2D game framework that was first released in September 2013 with iOS 7. It is an animation and graphics rendering framework that gives you the power to easily animate textured images, play video, render text, and add particle effects. It also includes an integrated physics library. SpriteKit is the first-ever game engine formally built into the iOS SDK.

In this chapter you will learn what SpriteKit is and how to create a new SpriteKit game using Xcode. You will then move on and create the beginnings of a SpriteKit game starting from scratch. You'll learn about SKNodes and their subclasses and you'll use an SKSpriteNode to add both a background node and a player node to your game.

## What You Need to Know and Have

This section of this book assumes you have a basic understanding of how to build iPhone applications using Xcode and the Xcode Simulator. It also assumes you have a basic knowledge of the iOS/Mac programming language Swift. If you are not familiar with Swift, there is a brief introduction in the appendix at the back of this book.

This book doesn't cover how to program. It focuses only on SpriteKit game programming.

To complete all the examples in the book, you will need to have an Intel-based Macintosh running OS X 10.11 (El Capitan) or newer. You will also need Xcode 8+ installed. You can find both of these in the Apple App Store.

## Introducing SuperSpaceMan

We feel the best way to learn anything is to do it. Therefore, in this book you are going to dive right in and create your own game. You will start off with the basic code for a 2D game, and you will add new features to the game as we introduce new topics with each chapter. At the end of the book, you will have a complete game.

© James Goodwill and Wesley Matlock 2017
J. Goodwill and W. Matlock, *Beginning Swift Games Development for iOS*,
DOI 10.1007/978-1-4842-2310-9_1

The game you are going to create is inspired by Sega's popular Sonic Jump Fever (https://itunes.apple.com/us/app/sonic-jump-fever/id794528112?mt=8). It is a vertical scroller that accelerates the main character through obstacles and collectables, increasing your score as you collect rings.

This game is similar in that it is a vertical scroller, but your main character is going to be a spaceman who hurtles through space collecting power orbs while trying to avoid black holes that will destroy him.

# Creating a Swift SpriteKit Project

Before you can get started, you will need to create a Swift SpriteKit project. Open Xcode and complete the following steps:

1. Click File ➤ New ➤ Project.

2. Select iOS.

3. Select the Game icon from the Application group. The choose template dialog should look like Figure 1-1.

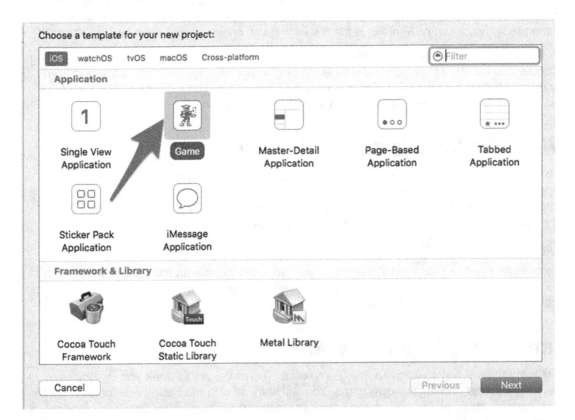

*Figure 1-1. The choose template dialog*

4. To move on, click the Next button.

5. Enter **SuperSpaceMan** for Product Name, **Apress** for Organization Name, and **com.apress** for Organization Identifier.

6. Make sure that Swift is the selected language, SpriteKit is the selected game technology, and iPhone is the selected device.

7. Before you click Next, look at Figure 1-2. If everything looks like that, click Next and select a good place to store your project files. Click Create.

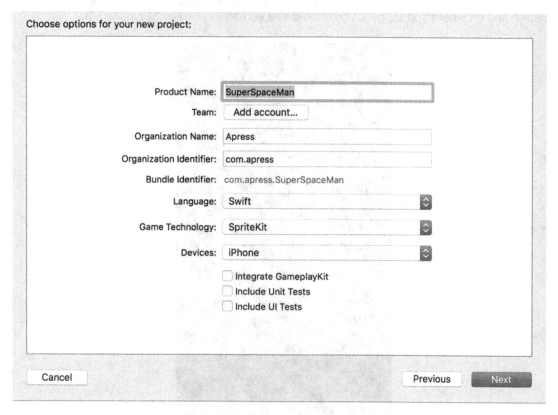

*Figure 1-2. The choose project options dialog*

> **Note**   You will notice you are creating an iPhone-only game. That's only because the game you are creating lends itself better to the iPhone. Everything we cover in this book translates to the iPad just as well.

You now have a working SpriteKit project. Go ahead and click the Play button to see what you have created. If everything went OK, you will see your new app running in the simulator.

**Note**   The Xcode simulator may take a while to start on some slower machines. Simulating SpriteKit apps can be very taxing on your processors.

It doesn't do a whole lot yet, but there is more to it than displaying "Hello, World!" Tap the simulator screen a few times. You will see rotating boxes displayed wherever you tap. Depending on where you tapped, you should see something similar to Figure 1-3.

*Figure 1-3. The SpriteKit sample application*

# Starting from Scratch

Although the standard SpriteKit template works great, you are going to be starting from scratch. Starting from nothing will allow you to see all the working parts in a SpriteKit game and will give you a much better understanding of what you are creating.

The first thing you need to do is make sure your game runs only in portrait mode. To do that, follow these steps:

1. Select the SuperSpaceMan project in the Project Explorer.

2. Then select SuperSpaceMan from Targets.

3. Deselect Landscape Left and Landscape Right.

At this point, your target settings should look like Figure 1-4.

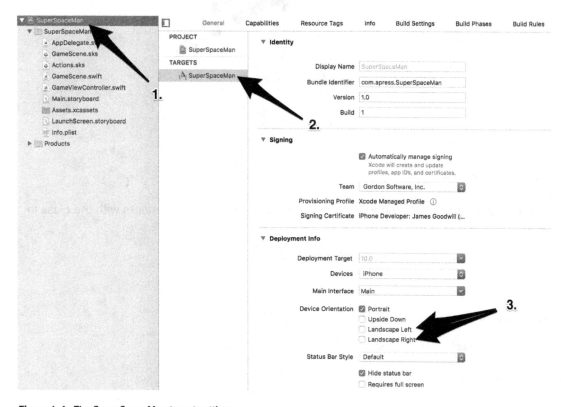

**Figure 1-4.** *The SuperSpaceMan target settings*

The next thing you need to do is delete the GameScene.sks and Actions.sks files. You will not be using the level editor in this book. You can find these files in the SuperSpaceMan group, as shown in Figure 1-5.

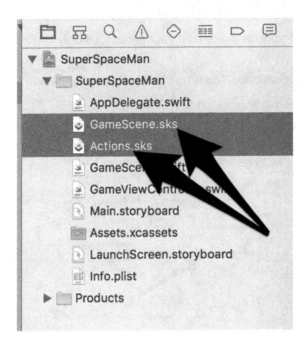

*Figure 1-5.  Delete the SKS files*

After you delete these files, open GameScene.swift and replace its contents with the class in Listing 1-1.

*Listing 1-1.  GameScene.swift: The SuperSpaceMan Main GameScene*

```swift
import SpriteKit

class GameScene: SKScene {

    required init?(coder aDecoder: NSCoder) {

        super.init(coder: aDecoder)
    }

    override init(size: CGSize) {

        super.init(size: size)

        backgroundColor = SKColor(red: 0.0, green: 0.0, blue: 0.0, alpha: 1.0)
    }
}
```

There is one more change you need to make before examining your baseline project. Open GameViewController.swift and replace its contents with the Listing 1-2 version of the same class.

*Listing 1-2. GameViewController.swift: The SuperSpaceMan Main UIViewController*

```
import SpriteKit

class GameViewController: UIViewController {

    var scene: GameScene!

    override var prefersStatusBarHidden: Bool {
        return true
    }

    override func viewDidLoad() {

        super.viewDidLoad()

        // 1. Configure the main view
        let skView = view as! SKView
        skView.showsFPS = true

        // 2. Create and configure our game scene
        scene = GameScene(size: skView.bounds.size)
        scene.scaleMode = .aspectFill

        // 3. Show the scene.
        skView.presentScene(scene)
    }
}
```

Save all your changes and click the Play button once more. Wow, um, that was not very exciting. If you made all the changes, you should now be staring at a totally black screen with only the current frame rate displayed. This was the intent. You truly are starting from nothing.

Let's take a moment and examine each component of your new game. First, open Main. storyboard. Everything here should look pretty normal. You should see a single storyboard with a single UIViewController. Expand Game View Controller Scene in the Storyboard Explorer and select Game View Controller, as shown in Figure 1-6.

*Figure 1-6.* *Game View Controller Scene*

Now expand the Utilities view on the right side of Xcode and click the "Show the Identity inspector" button. You will see the custom class of this UIViewController is your GameViewController.swift. Figure 1-7 shows you this connection.

*Figure 1-7.* *The custom class GameViewController*

There is one last thing to look at before you get back to the code portion of this tour. Go back to the Utilities view and select the Connections inspector. Notice the View outlet is connected to your GameViewController.view. Figure 1-8 shows this connection.

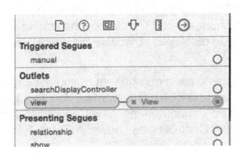

*Figure 1-8.* *The View outlet*

The point of going through this examination of the storyboard is to show that although SpriteKit is used to create games, the technology used to create games is just like what you would use to create any modern iOS app.

# The GameViewController Class

Let's get back to the code. You can ignore AppDelegate.swift—it's the same boilerplate code you use to start all iOS Swift applications. GameViewController.swift is the best starting point. We included it earlier, but for the sake of convenience, here it is again:

```
import SpriteKit

class GameViewController: UIViewController {

    var scene: GameScene!

    override var prefersStatusBarHidden: Bool {

        return true
    }

    override func viewDidLoad() {

        super.viewDidLoad()

        // 1. Configure the main view
        let skView = view as! SKView
        skView.showsFPS = true

        // 2. Create and configure our game scene
        scene = GameScene(size: skView.bounds.size)
        scene.scaleMode = .aspectFill

        // 3. Show the scene.
        skView.presentScene(scene)
    }
}
```

Starting with the first line of this controller, you see a simple import including the SpriteKit framework. This line makes all the SpriteKit-related classes available to your GameViewController. After that, you have a standard class definition—the GameViewController extends a UIViewController.

After the class definition, you see the declaration of the optional variable scene, which is declared as the type GameScene. GameScene is the class that will be doing most of your work. It is where you will be adding the game logic. We will look at this class in the next section.

Notice one thing about the scene variable: it's an optional. You know it's an optional because an exclamation point (!) follows its declaration. You declared this variable as an optional because you are not going to initialize it until the viewDidLoad() method fires and Swift requires you to initialize all properties in a class either at their declaration or in the init().

If you don't initialize a property in either of these locations, then you must declare the property as optional. We will use optionals throughout the examples in this book.

After the scene declaration, you see an override of the UIViewController's viewDidLoad() method. Here you return true because you don't want a status bar displayed in the game.

The next thing to check out is the viewDidLoad() method. This is where you really start to see your first active SpriteKit code. The first thing you do after calling super.viewDidLoad() is configure your main view. In the first step, you downcast your standard UIView to an SKView. The SKView is the view that will host your game scene mentioned earlier. For the most part, the SKView acts much like any UIView, with the exception that it has a collection of game-related properties and utility methods like the line following the downcast:

```
skView.showsFPS = true
```

This property of the SKView is used to show or hide the frames per second the application is rendering—the higher, the better.

After configuring the main view, you create and configure the GameScene:

```
scene = GameScene(size: skView.bounds.size)
scene.scaleMode = .aspectFill
```

The first line creates a new instance of the GameScene initializing the size to match the size of the view that will host the scene. After that, you set scaleMode to aspectFill. The scaleMode (implemented by the enum SKSceneScaleMode) is used to determine how the scene will be scaled to match the view that will contain it. Table 1-1 describes each of the available scaleMode properties.

*Table 1-1. The SKSceneScaleModes*

| SKSceneScaleMode | Definition |
| --- | --- |
| SKSceneScaleMode.fill | The fill scaleMode will fill the entire SKView without consideration to the ratio of width to height. |
| SKSceneScaleMode.aspectFill | The aspectFill mode will scale the scene to fill the hosting SKView while maintaining the aspect ratio of the scene, but there may be some cropping if the hosting SKView's aspect ratio is different. This is the mode you are using in this game. |
| SKSceneScaleMode.aspectFit | The aspectFit mode will scale the scene to fill the hosting SKView while maintaining the aspect ratio of the scene, but there may be some letterboxing if the hosting SKView's aspect ratio is different. |
| SKSceneScaleMode.resizeFill | The resizeFill mode will modify the size of the scene to fit the hosting view exactly. |

> **Note**   When setting the `scaleMode` property of the scene, you are using a shortened syntax
> to represent the mode you are setting, specifically the `.aspectFill` mode. You can use this dot
> syntax because you know the type of the `scaleMode` property is an `SKSceneScaleMode`, which
> is an enum containing all the scale modes.

Once you have the view and the scene configured, there is only one last thing to do: present
the scene. This is done with the last line in `viewDidLoad()`:

```
skView.presentScene(scene)
```

## The GameScene Class

Now that we'have walked you through each line of the `GameViewController` class, it is time
to talk about the `GameScene` class. Again, for convenience's sake, we're including the source
for the `GameScene.swift` file a second time:

```
import SpriteKit

class GameScene: SKScene {

    required init?(coder aDecoder: NSCoder) {

        super.init(coder: aDecoder)
    }

    override init(size: CGSize) {

        super.init(size: size)

        backgroundColor = SKColor(red: 0.0, green: 0.0, blue: 0.0, alpha: 1.0)
    }
}
```

As you look over `GameScene`, you will notice there's really not much to it. It extends `SKScene`
and implements two `init()` methods; the first `init()` that takes an `NSCoder` can be ignored.
The `init()` you are interested in is the second method, which takes a `CGSize` parameter
that represents the size you want the scene to be (in this case, the size you passed in from
the `GameViewController`). After that, you pass the size to your superclass and then set the
background color to black.

Although there's not a whole lot to your current `GameScene`, this is where you will be doing
almost all of your SpriteKit work. `SKScenes` and the classes that extend them are the root
nodes of all SpriteKit content, and your `GameScene` will grow considerably as you move along
in this book.

# Adding a Background and Player Sprite

We've talked enough for one chapter. Let's get back to the game itself. In this, the last section of this chapter, you are going to just jump in and add a game background and a player sprite to your scene and see how they look.

Before you can do this, you need some image files. You can find all the necessary assets for this book in the file assets.zip at www.apress.com (search for the title of this book). Go ahead and download and unzip this file.

Inside the unzipped folder you will find two folders: one is named Images, and another is named sprites.atlas. Copy the entire sprites.atlas folder directly into the SuperSpaceMan folder of the same project.

Next, open the Assets.xcassets folder in Xcode. You will see something similar to Figure 1-9.

*Figure 1-9.  Adding image assets*

Now select the Spaceship asset and delete it. After that, using Finder, browse to the Images folder in the previously downloaded zip file. Select the four folders inside the Images directory and drag them onto the xcassets palette directly below the Spaceship asset. When the files have been added, your xcassets palette will look like Figure 1-10.

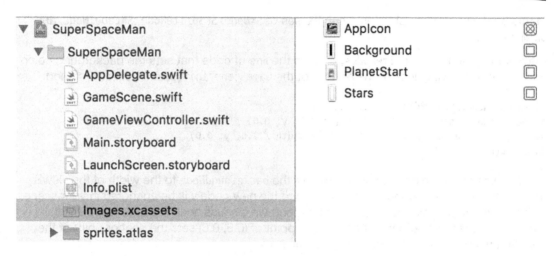

**Figure 1-10.** *The added image assets*

Now that you have all the images added to your project, let's put some of them to good use. Go back to GameScene.swift and add the following two lines to the beginning of the GameScene class:

```
let backgroundNode = SKSpriteNode(imageNamed: "Background")
let playerNode = SKSpriteNode(imageNamed: "Player")
```

Here you are adding two constants, backgroundNode and playerNode, both of which are being initialized to their respective images in the Image.xcassets folder.

Notice the type of each of these constants: they are both SKSpriteNodes. SKSpriteNode is a descendent of an SKNode, which is the primary building block of almost all SpriteKit content. SKNode itself does not draw any visual elements, but all visual elements in SpriteKit-based applications are drawn using SKNode subclasses. Table 1-2 defines the main descendants of SKNode that render visual elements.

**Table 1-2.** *The Descendants of SKNode That Render Visual Elements*

| Class | Description |
| --- | --- |
| SKSpriteNode | A node that is used to draw textured sprites |
| SKVideoNode | A node that presents video content |
| SKLabelNode | A node that is used to draw text strings |
| SKShapeNode | A node that is used to draw a shape based upon a Core Graphics path |
| SKEmitterNode | A node that is used to create and render particles |
| SKCropNode | A node that is used to crop child nodes using a mask |
| SKEffectNode | A node that is used to apply Core Image filters to its child nodes |

In this book you will be using three subclasses of SKNode: SKSpriteNode, SKLabelNode, and SKEmitterNode.

After adding the two SKSpriteNodes, remove the line of code that sets the background color and add the following lines to the bottom of the GameScene.init(size: CGSize) method:

```
backgroundNode.size.width = frame.size.width
backgroundNode.anchorPoint = CGPoint(x: 0.5, y: 0.0)
backgroundNode.position = CGPoint(x: size.width / 2.0, y: 0.0)
addChild(backgroundNode)
```

The first line of this snippet sets the width of the backgroundNode to the width of the view's frame. The next line of code determines where the new node will be anchored in your scene. Don't worry too much about this at the moment; we discuss anchor points in great detail in the next chapter. Just know that the anchor point of (0.5, 0.0) sets the anchor point of the background node to the bottom center of the node.

Next, you set the position of the backgroundNode. Here you are setting the node's position to an x-coordinate half the width of the scene, which is in the middle of the scene, and setting the y-coordinate to 0.0, which is the bottom of the scene.

The final line in the snippet adds the backgroundNode to your scene. To see what you have just accomplished, save your work and run the application again. You should now see your background displayed, as shown in Figure 1-11.

*Figure 1-11. The backgroundNode added to the GameScene*

That was easy enough. Now, let's add your player to your scene. Adding the player node is just as easy as adding the background. Take a look at the following snippet:

```
playerNode.position = CGPoint(x: size.width / 2.0, y: 80.0)
addChild(playerNode)
```

As you can see, this snippet is setting the position of the playerNode and adding it to the scene. Notice one difference here. You did not set the anchor point of the playerNode. That's because the default anchor point of all SKNodes is (0.5, 0.5), which is the center of the node. Again, don't worry about the positions or anchorPoints for now. We discuss them in the next chapter.

Go ahead and add this snippet to the bottom of the GameScene.init() method and save your changes. Now run the application one more time. You will now see the SuperSpaceMan positioned in front of the previously added backgroundNode, as shown in Figure 1-12.

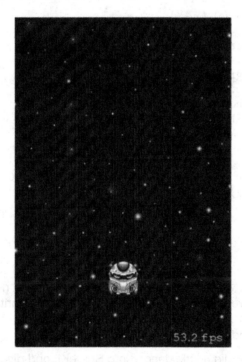

*Figure 1-12. The playerNode added to the GameScene*

After making these changes, your new GameScene.swift file should look like Listing 1-3.

*Listing 1-3. GameScene.swift: The Modified GameScene.swift*

```
import SpriteKit

class GameScene: SKScene {

    let backgroundNode = SKSpriteNode(imageNamed: "Background")
    let playerNode = SKSpriteNode(imageNamed: "Player")

    required init?(coder aDecoder: NSCoder) {

        super.init(coder: aDecoder)
    }

    override init(size: CGSize) {

        super.init(size: size)

        // adding the background
        backgroundNode.size.width = frame.size.width
        backgroundNode.anchorPoint = CGPoint(x: 0.5, y: 0.0)
        backgroundNode.position = CGPoint(x: size.width / 2.0, y: 0.0)
        addChild(backgroundNode)

        // add the player
        playerNode.position = CGPoint(x: size.width / 2.0, y: 80.0)
        addChild(playerNode)
    }
}
```

# Summary

In this chapter you learned what SpriteKit is and how you create a new SpriteKit game using Xcode. You then dove in and created the beginnings of a SpriteKit game starting from scratch. You learned about SKNodes and their subclasses and you used an SKSpriteNode to add both a background node and a player node.

In the next chapter, you will dig a little deeper into SpriteKit and discuss the details of the SKScene, including the coordinate system and anchor points. You will also look at how a scene's node tree is constructed.

# Chapter 2

# SpriteKit Scenes and SKNode Positioning

Chapter 1 talked about what SpriteKit was and how you can use it to create 2D games. It showed how to start working with the SKSpriteNode to create a background and player sprite and then showed how to add them to a game scene.

This chapter steps back a bit for a deeper look at SpriteKit scenes, including how scenes are built and why the order they are built in can change your game. We close the chapter with a discussion of SpriteKit coordinate systems and anchor points as they relate to SKNodes.

## What Is an SKScene?

We used the SKScene object in Chapter 1 to host the background and player nodes, but we really didn't explain the scene we were using. We just used it to add the sprites and called it a day. It's now time to dig in and see how SKScene really works. We'll start by defining an SKScene object.

An SKScene object represents a scene of content in a SpriteKit game. It inherits from SKEffectNode, SKNode, UIResponder, and, of course, NSObject. It is constructed first by creating the scene and then by adding *n* number of other SKNodes to it. The scene and all its child nodes are called the *node tree*, and the scene is the *root* of the node tree. The nodes contained in a scene provide the content the scene will animate and render for display.

The following are the steps you performed in the previous chapter to create the node tree. They are the basic steps you will complete whenever setting up a game scene:

1. Create the GameViewController.

2. Have the GameViewController create its UIView.

© James Goodwill and Wesley Matlock 2017
J. Goodwill and W. Matlock, *Beginning Swift Games Development for iOS*,
DOI 10.1007/978-1-4842-2310-9_2

3.  Inside the GameViewController.viewDidLoad(), downcast the UIView to an SKView and set the showFPS property to true:

    ```
    let skView = view as! SKView
    skView.showsFPS = true
    ```

4.  Create an instance of the SKScene named GameScene, passing it its size in the constructor and setting the scaleMode property:

    ```
    scene = GameScene(size: skView.bounds.size)
    scene.scaleMode = .aspectFill
    ```

5.  Inside the init() of the GameScene, update the backgroundNode and playerNode objects in the scene:

    ```
    backgroundNode.anchorPoint = CGPoint(x: 0.5, y: 0.0)
    backgroundNode.position = CGPoint(x: size.width / 2.0, y: 0.0)
    addChild(backgroundNode)

    playerNode.position = CGPoint(x: size.width / 2.0, y: 80.0)
    addChild(playerNode!)
    ```

6.  Present the complete scene in the GameViewController.viewDidLoad() method:

    ```
    skView.presentScene(scene)
    ```

At this point, you have a complete scene with a complete node tree. You can always add more nodes as the game progresses, but these are the basic steps that you will complete whenever you create a new SKScene.

# The SKScene Rendering Loop

In this section, we describe what happens after the SKScene is presented by the SKView. In a more traditional iOS application, you would render the view's content only once, and it would stay static until the model that the view is presenting changes. This is fine for a business app, but a game has the potential to constantly change.

Because of this dynamic characteristic, SpriteKit is constantly updating the scene and its contents. This constant updating is called the *rendering loop* (see Figure 2-1).

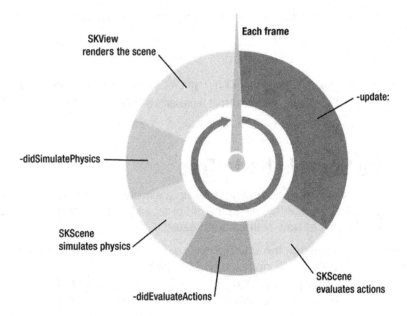

**Figure 2-1.** *The SpriteKit rendering loop*

Each iteration of this loop generates the next frame in the scene. The steps involved in generating the next frame of a scene are as follows:

1. The scene calls its update() method. This is where you will have most of your game logic. More often than not, you will be moving nodes around, adding new actions to existing nodes, and handling user input. (We talk about the update() method in Chapter 4.)

2. The scene next performs all programmed actions on its children. In this step, the scene executes any actions you may have set up in step 1. (We talk about actions in Chapter 5.)

3. The scene then calls the didEvaluateActions() method. This is where you would put any post-action game logic. An example would be testing the position of a node, after the actions were performed, and responding accordingly.

4. Next the scene executes any physics simulations on physics bodies in the scene. (We discuss physics in Chapter 3.)

5. The scene calls the didSimulatePhysics() method. This is much like the didEvaluateActions() method in that this is where you would add any game logic to be performed after all the physics simulations are completed. This is your last chance to perform any game logic before the scene is rendered.

6. The scene is rendered.

You will see examples of each step in the rendering loop as you progress through each chapter of this book.

> **Note**   When you have showsFPS in your SKView, you will see how many frames your game is rendering per second. Each frame being rendered represents a single iteration of the render loop.

# Building the Scene's Node Tree

Earlier in this chapter, we discussed how you set up a simple SKScene with a background node and a player node. You did this using the SKScene.addChild() method. This section takes a more in-depth look at how scenes are created.

We also mentioned the types that the SKScene class extends. One of those types is SKNode. SKNode is the class that holds all the nodes in an SKScene object's node tree. It also defines the methods that are used to manipulate this node tree. The most common of these methods are addChild(), insertChild(), and removeFromParent(), as described in Table 2-1.

*Table 2-1. The SKNode Node Tree Manipulating Methods*

| Method | Purpose |
|---|---|
| **addChild()** | The addChild(_:) method adds a node to the end of the receiver's collection of child nodes. |
| **insertChild(_:at:)** | The insertChild(_:at:) method inserts a child node at a specific position in the receiver's collection of child nodes. |
| **removeFromParent()** | removeFromParent() removes the receiving node from its parent. |

These are the three methods you will use to build the scene's node tree. The easiest way to see how these methods work is through a simple example. Take a look at the following sequence:

```
var gameScene = SKScene(size: CGSizeMake(320.0, 568.0))

var node1 = SKSpriteNode()
var node2 = SKSpriteNode()
var node3 = SKSpriteNode()

gameScene.addChild(node1)
gameScene.addChild(node2)
gameScene.addChild(node3)
```

Here you are creating an SKScene named gameScene. You then create three nodes and add them to the gameScene. At this point, the gameScene's node tree looks like Figure 2-2.

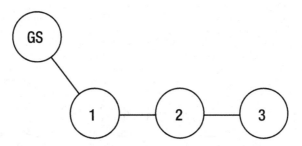

*Figure 2-2. The gameScene's children property after adding three nodes*

**Note**    The line in Figure 2-2 and several subsequent figures represents the order in which each node was added. It does not indicate that the nodes themselves are related to each other. For example, node2 was not added to node1. node2 was just added after node1.

At this point, the node tree contains three nodes: node1, node2, and node3 (in that order). Now, if you executed the following snippet, you would have a node tree that looked like Figure 2-3:

```
var node4 = SKSpriteNode()
gameScene.insertChild(node4, at: 2)
```

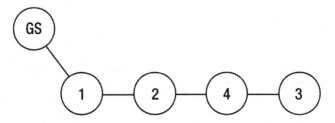

*Figure 2-3. The gameScene's node tree after inserting a fourth node*

The insertChild() method inserts a node at the given location in the node tree. In this case you're saying to insert the node into the third position (the first node being located at position 0). The children property now contains four nodes, with node4 being inserted between node2 and node3. Let's do one last thing and remove a node:

```
node2.removeFromParent()
```

By invoking node2's removeFromParent method, you have removed node2 from its parent, which is gameScene in this case. Now the node tree looks like Figure 2-4.

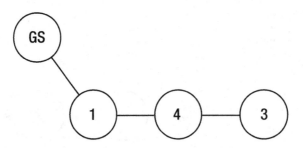

*Figure 2-4.  The gameScene's node tree after removing node4*

There is one last thing you need to look at, and that is nested nodes. Because the node tree
is part of SKNode, and because SKSpriteNode is extended from SKNode, it can have nested
nodes. The nice thing about nesting related nodes is that when you change the parent node,
the same changes will be applied to all the child nodes.

To see how nested nodes are represented in the node tree, let's go back to the node tree
represented by Figure 2-4. If you want to nest additional nodes inside node4, you can do so by
executing the following snippet right after the previously executed node2.removeFromParent().
Figure 2-5 represents the results of this snippet:

```
var node4a = SKSpriteNode()
var node4b = SKSpriteNode()
var node4c = SKSpriteNode()

node4.addChild(node4a)
node4.addChild(node4b)
node4.addChild(node4c)
```

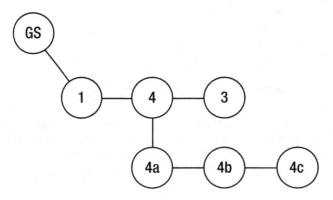

*Figure 2-5.  The gameScene's node tree with nodes nested inside node4*

# Rendering the Node Tree

Now that you know how to build the node tree, it's time to look at how the node tree is
rendered. The order in which you add nodes to your scene is important. When the scene
is rendered at the end of the rendering loop, it's rendered in reverse order of the way it was

built. Let's use the node tree represented by Figure 2-3 as an example. When this node tree is rendered, the scene will render each node in the following order:

1. node3
2. node4
3. node2
4. node1

Notice the last node rendered was the first node added to the scene. Nested nodes are also rendered in the reverse order of how they were added. If you were to render the node tree represented by Figure 2-5, it would be rendered in the following order:

1. node3
2. node4
   a. node4c
   b. node4b
   c. node4a
3. node1

This is important because, based on the position of each node, there could be some overlapping of nodes in the scene, which could lead to partial or completely hidden nodes.

It's also important because of the way SpriteKit performs hit testing. When SpriteKit processes a touch event or mouse event, it walks the scene to find the closest node that wants to receive the event. If the first node doesn't want the event, SpriteKit checks the next closest node and repeats this process until the event is handled or ignored. Just like the scene-rendering order, the order in which hit testing is performed is the reverse of the drawing order.

To see how this looks using the sample app, replace the current contents of the GameScene. init() method with the following code:

```
super.init(size: size)

backgroundColor = SKColor(red: 0.0, green: 0.0, blue: 0.0, alpha: 1.0)

// adding the background
backgroundNode.anchorPoint = CGPoint(x: 0.5, y: 0.0)
backgroundNode.position = CGPoint(x: size.width / 2.0, y: 0.0)
addChild(backgroundNode)

// add the player
let playerNode1 = SKSpriteNode(imageNamed: "Player")
playerNode1.position = CGPoint(x: size.width / 2.0, y: 80.0)
addChild(playerNode1)

let playerNode2 = SKSpriteNode(imageNamed: "Player")
playerNode2.position = CGPoint(x: size.width / 2.0, y: 100.0)
addChild(playerNode2)
```

```
let playerNode3 = SKSpriteNode(imageNamed: "Player")
playerNode3.position = CGPoint(x: size.width / 2.0, y: 120.0)
addChild(playerNode3)
```

In this snippet, three player nodes are being added to the scene, each of them 20 points below the most recently added node. To see the results, run the project again. You will see the overlapping players, with the first player added on top, as shown in Figure 2-6.

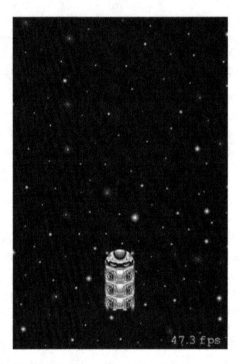

*Figure 2-6. The gameScene's with overlapping player nodes*

# Searching the Node Tree

There is one last topic we want to cover before moving on to the coordinate system and anchor points: how you search the node tree. Something we've not discussed yet is the name property of the SKNode. The SKNode.name property is a String property that can be used to identify a unique sprite or a group of sprites.

An example of this would be to give the unique playerNode a name of Player. Assuming you were inside the GameScene and you did give the playerNode a name of Player, you could then search the GameScene for a unique node named Player using the following line of code:

```
childNode(withName: "Player")
```

This method returns an optional SKNode. If more than one child shares the same name, then the first node in the children array would be returned. If no child with this name was found, then return would have no value.

Another example might be to name a collection of sprites with the same name. For example, you could name a collection of sprites with the same circular texture, such as orb. You could then search for all sprites with that name and apply the set of actions in one call. You can do this using SKNode's enumerateChildNodes(withName: using:) method.

This method searches for all nodes with the passed-in name and then executes the code in the block on each node found. Again, assuming you were inside the GameScene and you've added several sprites all named orb, you could search for all the orb nodes and execute a block on each one using the following snippet:

```
enumerateChildNodes(withName: "orb", using: {
    node, stop in
    // do something with node or stop
})
```

Everything looks pretty straightforward here except for the parameters being passed to the block every time a node with the name orb is found. The first parameter is a reference to the node that was found—no problem. The second parameter, stop, is a pointer to a Boolean that can be used to stop the iteration. If you want to stop iterating over each node found, set the stop parameter's memory property to true, as in the following example.

```
stop.memory = true
```

# Looking at SKSpriteNode Coordinates and Anchor Points

So far, we've talked about how you create an SKScene object and how it is rendered. We're now going to talk about how you position nodes in a scene. Let's begin by looking at the scene's coordinate system. First, be sure to change the GameScene.init() method back to the following:

```
init(size: CGSize) {

    super.init(size: size)

    backgroundColor = SKColor(red: 0.0, green: 0.0, blue: 0.0, alpha: 1.0)

    // adding the background
    backgroundNode.anchorPoint = CGPoint(x: 0.5, y: 0.0)
    backgroundNode.position = CGPoint(x: size.width / 2.0, y: 0.0)
    addChild(backgroundNode)

    // add the player
    playerNode.position = CGPoint(x: size.width / 2.0, y: 80.0)
    addChild(playerNode)
}
```

# Coordinates

When a scene is first initialized, its size property is set in its initializer, as you saw earlier. The size of the scene denotes the size of the visible portion of the scene. It doesn't define the entire size of the game world. You can think of the size of the scene as the viewport into the game world.

By default, an SKScene's origin is placed in the bottom-left corner of the view presenting it. The coordinate representing this origin is (0, 0). Going back to the game from the previous chapter, add this line of code to the GameScene.init() method immediately following the call to the super.init():

```
print("The size is (\(size)")
```

Now run the application again using the iPhone 6s simulator. After you do, look in the console window. You will see the following output:

```
The size is: (375.0, 667.0).
```

This is the size of the scene running on an iPhone 6s. You can try this again, running on either the iPhone SE or 6+ simulators. These values tell you the size of your scene (the viewport into your game world).

If you want to position SKNode objects into the visible world of your game, you have to set their positions inside the range of (0, 0) to (375, 667) on the iPhone 6s or from (0, 0) to (320, 568) on the iPhone SE. Take a moment and play around with the coordinate system. Go back to the GameScene.init() method and change the position of the playerNode using the following line:

```
playerNode.position = CGPoint(x: size.width / 2, y: size.height / 2)
```

With this change, you are positioning the playerNode in the center of the scene. To see the position change, run the app in the simulator again. You will now see your player in the middle of your scene, as shown in Figure 2-7.

*Figure 2-7. The playerNode in the middle of the scene*

Make one more position change before you move on. Change playerNode's position using the following line of code:

```
playerNode.position = CGPoint(x: size.width, y: size.height)
```

As you can see, the new position is set to the maximum (x, y) of the viewable area in the scene. Run the app in the simulator again. You will see your player in the upper-right corner of your scene, as shown in Figure 2-8.

*Figure 2-8. The playerNode at the top right of the scene*

Although you successfully positioned your player in the upper-right corner of the scene, you will notice something a little odd—only the bottom-left quarter of the playerNode is visible. You will see why this is the case in the next section when we focus on anchor points.

## Anchor Points

As you saw in the previous section, when you positioned the playerNode in the top-right corner of the scene, only the bottom-left quarter of the node was visible in the scene. That's because the default anchor point for SKSpriteNodes is positioned at the center of the node.

A sprite's anchorPoint property is used to set the point in the SKSpriteNode's frame in which the sprite's position property will be applied. That sounds a little complicated, but it's really pretty straightforward. Take a look at Figure 2-9.

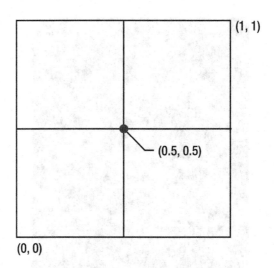

*Figure 2-9. SKSpriteNode's anchor point unit coordinate system*

This figure shows an SKSpriteNode's anchor point coordinate system. Notice the dot at position (0.5, 0.5). This is the default anchor point. Figure 2-10 shows some common anchor points.

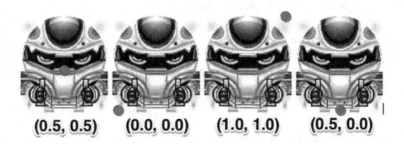

*Figure 2-10. SKSpriteNode example anchor points*

In Figure 2-10 there are four common anchor points as they relate to the sprites they're applied to. Looking at these examples, you can see that if you want to position the playerNode at the top-rightmost position of the scene and still have the entire spriteNode visible in the scene, you would need to set the sprite's anchorPoint property to (1.0, 1.0). Do that now by adding the following line of code directly after playerNode's construction:

```
playerNode.anchorPoint = CGPoint(x: 1.0, y: 1.0)
```

Now run the application once more. You will now see the entire playerNode positioned at the top right of the scene, as shown in Figure 2-11.

*Figure 2-11.* *The entire playerNode at the top right of the scene*

To get a handle on anchor points, play around with different anchor points and positions of the `playerNode` and see how each of the different anchor points affects the positioning of the `playerNode`. It's really important to understand how the `position` and `anchorPoint` properties work together.

> **Note**  When you're finished playing around with the `playerNode`'s position and anchor point, revert all your code changes until the project is back to where you left it in Chapter 1.

# Summary

This chapter covered quite a bit of information, including what `SKScenes` are and how they are built. We also talked about the `SKScene` rendering loop and how the order the scene's node tree is constructed can affect the look and interactivity of the nodes. We closed the chapter with a look at a scene's coordinate system and node anchor points.

Chapter 3 covers SpriteKit's physics engine and collision detection. That chapter will be a lot of fun, and you'll start seeing your game coming to life.

# Adding Physics and Collision Detection to Your Game

This chapter covers SpriteKit's physics engine and collision detection. We begin with a discussion of SKPhysicsBody—the class used to simulate collision detection. You will then turn on gravity in the game world and see how that affects the nodes. After that, you will add a touch responder to propel the playerNode up into space. I close this chapter with a discussion of how to handle node collisions.

## What Is an SKPhysicsBody?

To simulate physics in a SpriteKit game, you add a physics body to a scene or node. A physics body, implemented by the SpriteKit class SKPhysicsBody, is a simulated object attached to a node in the scene's node tree. The SKPhysicsBody class uses the properties of the node, such as the position and velocity, combined with its own properties, to simulate how physical forces are applied to the simulated game world. It does the calculations to perform these simulations with each iteration of the render loop.

There are three types of physics bodies: dynamic volume, a static volume, and an edge. A *dynamic volume* is a physical body with a volume and a mass that is affected by collisions and forces in the physics simulation. Nodes with a dynamic volume attached to them are the active nodes in games.

A physics body with a *static volume* is just like a dynamic volume, except forces and collisions don't affect them. Static volume bodies are often used as barriers in a game. When a dynamic body collides with a static body, the dynamic body is affected by the collision, and the static body remains constant.

An *edge* is a static body without volume. The simulation never moves an edge, and an edge's mass doesn't affect the simulation of other nodes. Edges represent negative space within a scene.

© James Goodwill and Wesley Matlock 2017
J. Goodwill and W. Matlock, *Beginning Swift Games Development for iOS*,
DOI 10.1007/978-1-4842-2310-9_3

# Adding Physics to Your Game World

The easiest way to see how all this works is to just do it. Let's begin by creating and associating an SKPhysicsBody with the playerNode. Add the following lines of code to the GameScene's .init(size: CGSize) method immediately following the construction of the playerNode:

```
playerNode.physicsBody = SKPhysicsBody(circleOfRadius: playerNode.size.width / 2)
playerNode.physicsBody?.isDynamic = true
```

Take a look at those two lines of code. The first line creates an SKPhysicsBody passing the initializer a parameter named circleOfRadius with a CGFloat for the value. SpriteKit provides a handful of standard shapes for physics bodies, including circles (circleOfRadius), rectangles (rectangleOfSize), and a path-based polygon (polygonFromPath). The most efficient of these shapes is the circle, and the most inefficient is the path-based polygon.

Because the circle is the most efficient node shape, it will be the shape used for all physics bodies in this game. The value passed to the constructor, in this instance, is the width of the playerNode divided by 2. We're using this value because we want to create a circle around the playerNode starting from its center with a radius of half the width of the node. This will result in a circle that surrounds the playerNode completely. If there were an SKPhysicsBody (circleOfDiameter:) constructor, then we wouldn't need to divide the width by 2, but there is no such constructor.

Let's get back to the second line of this snippet. The second line turns the playerNode into a physics body with a dynamic volume. It will now respond to gravity and other physical bodies in the scene. Once you have made these changes, your new player setup code should look like the following:

```
// add the player
playerNode.physicsBody = SKPhysicsBody(circleOfRadius: playerNode?.size.width / 2)
playerNode.physicsBody?.isDynamic = true

playerNode.position = CGPoint(x: size.width / 2.0, y: 80.0)
addChild(playerNode)
```

Now, go back to Xcode and run the application once again. If you weren't paying close attention, you would see only the background node of the game. This is because the default gravity setting in SpriteKit matches the earth's gravitational forces, and the player node is now falling rapidly toward the center of the earth.

To slow things down, you need to play around with the game world's gravity settings until you have a gravitational force you're happy with. Go back to the GameScene.init (size: CGSize) method, add the following line immediately following the super.init(size: size) invocation, and run the application again:

```
physicsWorld.gravity = CGVector(dx: 0.0, dy:  -0.1);
```

Now you will see the player slowly drift off the bottom of the screen. What you have done here is modify the world's gravity using the SKScene's physicsWorld.gravity property and set it to a value that slows the playerNode's descent considerably.

Notice the value you set the gravity property to is a vector with a value of 0.0 for the x-coordinate and a value of –0.1 for the y-coordinate. You set the x-coordinate to a value of 0.0 because gravity exerts force only along the y-axis. The result of this vector is a force that results in a gravitational force pulling toward the bottom of the scene.

Though setting the y-coordinate to –0.1 helps us see the playerNode fall off the scene, it's not practical for game play. A more reasonable value would be –2.0. Set the gravity property to CGVector(dx: 0.0, dy: -2.0) and try running it again. You'll see the player fall off the screen, but at a rate more conducive to game play.

> **Note** In this section you modified the world's gravity property to a value that's not consistent with the earth's real gravity. We had you do this because rather than trying to match the earth's gravity, you're trying to create a simulated game world that is fun for your players. You'll find yourself doing this often as you start creating your own games. After all, it's about your players having fun, not matching the real world.

# Applying Forces to SKPhysicsBody

At this point you have your player responding to the physical properties of your game world, and you've also adjusted the gravitational forces that pull the player off the bottom of the visible scene. This is great, but watching your character fall of the screen is not going to be a whole lot of fun. It's now time to apply some forces to the player to allow him to fight gravity and stay in the visible scene. The two most common methods of changing the velocity of an SKPhysicsBody are applying a force and applying an impulse.

When applying a force to an SKPhysicsBody, you apply the force for a length of time based on the amount of time that passes between invocations of the rendering loop. Forces are generally used for continuous velocity changes. You apply forces using the SKPhysicsBody's applyForce() method.

When you apply an impulse to an SKPhysicsBody, you're applying an instantaneous change to the body's velocity that is independent of the amount of simulation time that has passed. Impulses are used when you need to apply an immediate change to a node's velocity. You apply impulses using the SKPhysicsBody's applyImpulse() method. The game is going to use impulses to modify the player's velocity and will therefore use the applyImpulse() method.

Before you can apply an impulse to the player's physics body, you need to give the user the ability to tell the game when to apply the impulse. Because SKNode extends UIResponder and SKScene is an SKNode, you can test for touches in the scene by overriding the GameScene's UIResponder.touchesBegan() method. To do this, you need to complete two steps.

First, add the following line of code that turns on user interaction in the scene immediately before the line of code that creates your backgroundNode:

```
isUserInteractionEnabled = true
```

Then override the UIResponder.touchesBegan() by adding the following method to the GameScene class:

```
override func touchesBegan(_ touches: Set<UITouch>, with event: UIEvent?) {

    playerNode.physicsBody?.applyImpulse(CGVector(dx: 0.0,dy:  40.0))
}
```

Add this method to the bottom of the GameScene class definition and rerun the SuperSpaceMan application. While the application is running, tap the screen as many times as you need to get the player to fly back into the scene. The number of taps it takes will depend on how far the playerNode fell out of the scene.

After playing around with the touch responder, take a look at the single line of code in the touchesBegan() method. This line applies an impulse to the playerNode's physics body every time you tap the screen. The direction and strength of the impulse depend on the vector you pass to the applyImpulse() method. In this case, you're creating a vector with an x-value of 0.0 (because you want to apply the impulse only linearly along the y-axis) and a y-value of 40.0, which results in a pulse that springs the player in the opposite direction of gravity.

Before moving on, play around with the y-value used to create this vector. It will help you understand how this value affects the size of the pulse. When you're finished, put the y-value back to 40.0 and let's move on.

Once you have the player visible in the scene, tap the screen until the player is at the top of the visible scene and watch him fall. One thing to note about the way the playerNode descends is that the player falls as if it has no surface area to dampen its velocity. That doesn't look quite right.

To fix this problem, SpriteKit's SKPhysicsBody provides a linearDamping property. This property, which has a default of 0.1, is used to reduce a physics body's linear velocity to simulate fluid or air friction. In this case, you are simulating air friction. To see how you can use this property, add the following line of code immediately after the positioning of the playerNode and run the application again:

```
playerNode.physicsBody?.linearDamping = 1.0
```

Now tap the screen until the player reaches the top of the screen and let it fall once more. This time, the playerNode will fall more slowly, simulating the resistance of falling through air.

Before moving on to the collision-detection section of this chapter, make sure your modified GameScene.swift file looks like Listing 3-1.

*Listing 3-1. GameScene.swift: The SuperSpaceMan Main Modified GameScene*

```
import SpriteKit

class GameScene: SKScene {

    let backgroundNode = SKSpriteNode(imageNamed: "Background")
    let playerNode = SKSpriteNode(imageNamed: "Player")
```

```
required init?(coder aDecoder: NSCoder) {

    super.init(coder: aDecoder)
}

override init(size: CGSize) {

    super.init(size: size)

    physicsWorld.gravity = CGVector(dx: 0.0, dy: -2.0);

    backgroundColor = SKColor(red: 0.0, green: 0.0, blue: 0.0, alpha: 1.0)

    isUserInteractionEnabled = true

    // adding the background

    backgroundNode.size.width = frame.size.width
    backgroundNode.anchorPoint = CGPoint(x: 0.5, y: 0.0)
    backgroundNode.position = CGPoint(x: size.width / 2.0, y: 0.0)
    addChild(backgroundNode)

    // add the player
    playerNode.physicsBody = SKPhysicsBody(circleOfRadius: playerNode.size.width / 2)
    playerNode.physicsBody?.isDynamic = true

    playerNode.position = CGPoint(x: size.width / 2.0, y: 80.0)
    playerNode.physicsBody?.linearDamping = 1.0
    addChild(playerNode!)
}

override func touchesBegan(_ touches: Set<UITouch>, with event: UIEvent?) {

    playerNode.physicsBody?.applyImpulse(CGVector(dx: 0.0, dy: 40.0))
}
}
```

# Adding Collision Detection to Your SKNode

At this point, the game has a playerNode that responds to gravity and impulses; it's now time to add another node that your player can interact with. In this section, you're going to add another sprite that represents an orb in your game. You will begin by adding the orb and positioning it above the player. After that, you will modify the orb's properties so the player and orb interact naturally in the game. Finally, you will add code that will detect collisions between the player and the orb and remove the orb from the scene when they collide.

## Adding a Node to Collide Into

Let's get started. The first thing you're going to do is add the orb sprite to the GameScene at a position a little to the left of and above the player. The image you're going to use for the orb, in the sprites.atlas collection, is named PowerUp. There's nothing special about adding this sprite—you do so just like you added the player. First add the declaration of the new node to the GameScene immediately following the declaration of the playerNode:

```
let orbNode = SKSpriteNode(imageNamed: "PowerUp")
```

After adding the declaration of the orbNode, add this code to the end of the GameScene. init(size: CGSize) method:

```
orbNode.position = CGPoint(x: 150.0, y: size.height - 25)
orbNode.physicsBody = SKPhysicsBody(circleOfRadius: orbNode.size.width / 2)
orbNode.physicsBody?.isDynamic = false
addChild(orbNode)
```

As you look over this snippet, you'll see that it looks similar to the code you used to add the playerNode, with a couple exceptions. First, the orbNode is being positioned 25 points from the top of the scene and a little to the left of the player. The second thing to notice is that the orbNode.physicsBody.isDynamic property is being set to false. That's because you don't want this node to react to other nodes. You want the playerNode to pass through the scene collecting power-up orbs to fuel its ascent. This is why you've given the orbNode's physicsBody a static volume.

Go ahead and run the app again, but this time tap the screen until the playNode collides with the orbNode. Because the playerNode is a dynamic body, it bounces off and goes spinning into the distance, and because the orbNode is a static body, it remains constant.

This is pretty cool for so little coding. But before moving on to detecting the collision and removing the orb, you need to do one more thing. As you will have noticed when the playerNode collided with the orbNode, the playerNode started to spin. That's a correct response in a lot of cases, but for this game you want the playerNode to just keep blasting through the orbs without spinning off. SpriteKit provides a simple method of preventing these rotations: the physicsBody.allowsRotation property. Add the following line of code immediately before the playerNode is added to the scene:

```
playerNode.physicsBody?.allowsRotation = false
```

Now run the app again. This time when the player collides with the orb, it will bounce off but will not spin.

## Adding Collision Detection

You now have your playerNode and orbNode colliding and reacting to the collisions properly. It's time to add explicit code that will detect collisions between the player and the orb and remove the orb from the scene when they collide.

When you run your game, you do see the collision between the orb and player, but what you want to do now is detect when that collision occurs and remove the orb that was part of the collision. Later in the game you will be adding a fuel element so that the orbs will provide fuel for the player to ascend higher and higher.

To be able to detect when SKNodes come into contact with each other, you first implement the SpriteKit protocol SKPhysicsContactDelegate in the GameScene class and then implement the methods needed in your game. The SKPhysicsContactDelegate protocol defines two methods used to detect when SKNodes touch each other: the didBeginContact and the didEndContact() methods. The following snippet shows the protocol:

```
public protocol SKPhysicsContactDelegate : NSObjectProtocol {
    optional public func didBegin(_ contact: SKPhysicsContact)
    optional public func didEnd(_ contact: SKPhysicsContact)
}
```

The method names make their function pretty straightforward. The didBegin(_ contact: SKPhysicsContact) method is invoked when the contact first begins, and the didEnd(_ contact: SKPhysicsContact) method is invoked when contact ends. For this game, you're interested only in the first method, didBegin(_ contact: SKPhysicsContact), because you don't want the playerNode to pass through the orb. You want the orb to be removed from the scene as soon as the playerNode contacts the orb.

Go back to the GameScene.swift file, and you will create a class extension after the closing } for the GameScene class, add the following code snippet:

```
extension GameScene: SKPhysicsContactDelegate {

}
```

After you add the extension, add this implementation of the didBegin(_ contact: SKPhysicsContact) method to the end of the GameScene class:

```
func didBegin(_ contact: SKPhysicsContact) {
    print("There has been contact.")
}
```

Finally, you need to make the GameScene the delegate of the scene's physicsWorld.contactD elegate. Do that by adding the following line in the GameScene.init(size: CGSize) method directly after the call to the super.init(size: size):

```
physicsWorld.contactDelegate = self
```

# Adding Bit Masks to Your SKPhysicsBody

Everything is wired up to receive contact notifications, so the next thing you need to do is tell SpriteKit which objects you want to receive contact notifications. You do that using a concept called *bit masks*.

The SKPhysicsBody has three bit mask properties you can use to define the way your physics body interacts with other physics bodies in a game world: collisionBitMask, categoryBitMask, and contactTestBitMask. Each of these properties is described in Table 3-1.

*Table 3-1. The SKPhysicsBody's Three Bit Mask Properties*

| Method | Purpose |
|---|---|
| collisionBitMask | Defines the collision categories that your SKPhysicsBody will bump into. All other physics bodies will be passed through. |
| categoryBitMask | Defines the collision categories to which a physics body belongs. |
| contactTestBitMask | Determines which categories this physics body makes contact with. An example used in your game would be coming in contact with the orb. You want SpriteKit to tell you when the playerNode comes into contact with the orbNode. |

At the moment, the app has only two nodes: a player and an orb. This makes it easy to categorize them. You can put the player into the category CollisionCategoryPlayer and all the orb nodes (there is only one at the moment) into a category named CollisionCategoryPowerUpOrbs. These two category bit masks are defined here:

```
let CollisionCategoryPlayer   : UInt32 = 0x1 << 1
let CollisionCategoryPowerUpOrbs : UInt32 = 0x1 << 2
```

Here are two bit masks, CollisionCategoryPlayer and CollisionCategoryPowerUpOrbs, each of which is an unsigned 32-bit integer. This is important to note because collision bit masks are 32 bits, and you can have only 32 unique categories. Go ahead and add these two lines to the GameScene immediately following the declaration of the orbNode and before the first init() method:

```
let CollisionCategoryPlayer   : UInt32 = 0x1 << 1
let CollisionCategoryPowerUpOrbs : UInt32 = 0x1 << 2
```

Let's see how to set up the collision-detection properties using the two nodes. Let's start with the playerNode. The following three lines set up the player's collision properties:

```
playerNode.physicsBody?.categoryBitMask = CollisionCategoryPlayer
playerNode.physicsBody?.contactTestBitMask = CollisionCategoryPowerUpOrbs
playerNode.physicsBody?.collisionBitMask = 0
```

The first line associates the playerNode.physicsBody's category bit mask to the CollisionCategoryPlayer. The second line tells SpriteKit that whenever your physics body comes into contact with another physics body belonging to the category CollisionCategoryPowerUpOrbs, you want to be notified. The final line, setting the playerNode.physicsBody's collisionBitMask to 0, tells SpriteKit not to handle collisions for you. The game is going to be doing this itself in the didBegin () method. Go ahead and add these three lines to the GameScene.init(size: CGSize) method immediately after this line:

```
playerNode.physicsBody?.allowsRotation = false
```

Next, let's move on to configuring the orbNode's phsyicsBody. Setting up the orbNode's physics body is even easier than setting up the playerNode and can be done with only two lines of code:

```
orbNode.physicsBody?.categoryBitMask = CollisionCategoryPowerUpOrbs
orbNode.physicsBody?.collisionBitMask = 0
```

The first line associates the orbNode's physics body to the category CollisionCategoryPowerUpOrbs, and the second line, just like when configuring the player, is set to 0 because you're going to handle collisions yourself. There is one thing to note here. When configuring the orb node, you're not setting a contactTestBitMask because it's not necessary. You will be notified of the contact because you already set this up in the playerNode. Add these two lines to the GameScene.init(size: CGSize) method immediately before adding the orbNode to the scene:

```
orbNode.physicsBody?.categoryBitMask = CollisionCategoryPowerUpOrbs
orbNode.physicsBody?.collisionBitMask = 0
```

At this point, you have both nodes configured for collision detection, and whenever the playerNode comes into contact with the orbNode, the didBegin(_contact: SKPhysicsContact) method will be invoked. Let's give it a try. Save all your changes and run the application, paying attention to the console as you're tapping the screen. Now when the player comes into contact with the orb, you will see the following text printed in the console:

```
There has been contact.
```

Also, notice that this time the player passes through the orb. That's because you set the physics bodies' contactTestBitMask property to 0 in both nodes.

## Removing the Orb When You Receive a Contact Message

The last thing you're going to do is add the functionality needed to remove the orbNode when the playerNode comes into contact with it. To do that, you need to make a couple of changes. First, as mentioned in Chapter 2, SKNodes have a name property that is used to identify a single node or group of nodes, so you need to use this property to tell you that the player runs into an orb. To name the orbNode, add the following line of code to the GameScene.init(size: CGSize) method right before you add orbNode to the scene:

```
orbNode.name = "POWER_UP_ORB"
```

The last thing you need to do is modify the didBegin(_contact: SKPhysicsContact method to see whether the node being contacted by the player SKNode has a name property equal to POWER_UP_ORB and, if it does, remove the node from the scene. The modified didBegin (_contact: SKPhysicsContact) method is shown here:

```
func didBegin(_ contact: SKPhysicsContact) {

    let nodeB = contact.bodyB.node

    if nodeB?.name == "POWER_UP_ORB" {

        nodeB?.removeFromParent()
    }
}
```

The first thing to look at in this method is the parameter being passed to the method. Here you have a contact parameter with a type of SKPhysicsContact. The SKPhysicsContact contains all the information you need to handle a node contact. The SKPhysicsContact class contains five properties to help you determine the characteristics of the contact, defined in Table 3-2.

*Table 3-2. The SKPhysicsContact Properties*

| Method | Purpose |
|---|---|
| bodyA | The bodyA property, an SKPhysicsBody, represents first body in the contact. (This will be the playerNode.) |
| bodyB | The bodyB property, an SKPhysicsBody, represents second body in the contact. (This will be the orbNode.) |
| contactPoint | The contactPoint, a CGPoint, represents the contact point between the two physics bodies in the scene coordinates. |
| collisionImpulse | The contactImpulse, a CGFloat, specifies how hard these two bodies struck each other using newton-seconds as the unit of measure. |
| collisionNormal | The collisionNormal, a CGVector, specifies the direction of the collision. |

You're interested only in the second of these properties, bodyB. Getting back to the didBegin(_contact: SKPhysicsContact) method, notice the second line of the method. Here you are referencing the contact's bodyB property, which as we mentioned earlier is an SKPhysicsContact. Once you have this reference, you can then get the SKNode instance from the bodyB.node property, which represents the second node in the collision.

Once you have the second SKNode in the collision, you can check to see whether it has the name POWER_UP_ORB. If it does, you invoke the node's removeFromParent() method, which, as it sounds, removes the orbNode from the scene.

Go ahead and replace the contents of the current didBegin(_contact: SKPhysicsContact with this version and run the app one last time. This time, when the playerNode collides with the orbNode, the orbNode disappears from the scene.

At the end of this chapter, the new GameScene.swift should look like Listing 3-2.

*Listing 3-2. GameScene.swift: The SuperSpaceMan GameScene with Collision Detection*

```
import SpriteKit

class GameScene: SKScene {

    let backgroundNode = SKSpriteNode(imageNamed: "Background")
    let playerNode = SKSpriteNode(imageNamed: "Player")
    let orbNode = SKSpriteNode(imageNamed: "PowerUp")

    let CollisionCategoryPlayer : UInt32 = 0x1 << 1
    let CollisionCategoryPowerUpOrbs : UInt32 = 0x1 << 2
```

```
required init?(coder aDecoder: NSCoder) {

    super.init(coder: aDecoder)
}

override init(size: CGSize) {

    super.init(size: size)

    physicsWorld.contactDelegate = self

    physicsWorld.gravity = CGVector(dx: 0.0, dy: -2.0);

    backgroundColor = SKColor(red: 0.0, green: 0.0, blue: 0.0, alpha: 1.0)

    isUserInteractionEnabled = true

    // adding the background
    backgroundNode.size.width = frame.size.width
    backgroundNode.anchorPoint = CGPoint(x: 0.5, y: 0.0)
    backgroundNode.position = CGPoint(x: size.width / 2.0, y: 0.0)
    addChild(backgroundNode)

    // add the player
    playerNode.physicsBody = SKPhysicsBody(circleOfRadius: playerNode.size.width / 2)
    playerNode.physicsBody?.isDynamic = true

    playerNode.position = CGPoint(x: size.width / 2.0, y: 80.0)
    playerNode.physicsBody?.linearDamping = 1.0
    playerNode.physicsBody?.allowsRotation = false
    playerNode.physicsBody?.categoryBitMask = CollisionCategoryPlayer
    playerNode.physicsBody?.contactTestBitMask = CollisionCategoryPowerUpOrbs
    playerNode.physicsBody?.collisionBitMask = 0
    addChild(playerNode)

    orbNode.position = CGPoint(x: 150.0, y: size.height - 25)
    orbNode.physicsBody = SKPhysicsBody(circleOfRadius: orbNode.size.width / 2)
    orbNode.physicsBody?.isDynamic = false
    orbNode.physicsBody?.categoryBitMask = CollisionCategoryPowerUpOrbs
    orbNode.physicsBody?.collisionBitMask = 0
    orbNode.name = "POWER_UP_ORB"
    addChild(orbNode)
}

override func touchesBegan(_ touches: Set<UITouch>, with event: UIEvent?) {

    playerNode.physicsBody?.applyImpulse(CGVector(dx: 0.0, dy: 40.0))
}
}
```

```
extension GameScene: SKPhysicsContactDelegate {

    func didBegin(_ contact: SKPhysicsContact) {

        let nodeB = contact.bodyB.node

        if nodeB?.name == "POWER_UP_ORB" {

            nodeB?.removeFromParent()
        }
    }
}
```

# Summary

This chapter discussed SpriteKit's physics engine and collision detection. We began the chapter with a discussion of the `SKPhysicsBody`. You then turned on the game world's gravity, which pulled the player down the length of the scene. After that you added a touch responder to propel the `playerNode` back up into space. Finally, we closed the chapter with a discussion on how to handle collisions.

In Chapter 4, you will add scrolling to the scene so that the player can fly higher in the scene without flying off the top of the scene. You will also add accelerometer integration to give additional controls to the player.

# Adding Scene Scrolling and Game Control

In this chapter, you will start adding some real functionality to your game. You'll begin by making some small changes to the current GameScene. After that, you will add additional orb nodes to collide into. You will then add scrolling to your scene, allowing you to make it look like the player is flying through space collecting orbs. Finally, you will start using the phone's accelerometer to move the player along the x-axis.

## Reorganizing the GameScene

Before you move on to adding scrolling and the accelerometer, you need to do some small code changes in the existing GameScene. In previous chapters there was a lot of code that showed how to do certain things in SpriteKit. The changes you'll be making here are reorganizational changes focused on setting up the game for continued game development.

The first thing you need to change is the strength of gravity in the game's physics world. You are going to do this by changing the vector that represents gravity's force from (0.0, –2.0) to (0.0, –5.0). Go ahead and find where you set the physicsWorld.gravity property and change it to the following:

```
physicsWorld.gravity = CGVector(dx: 0.0, dy: -5.0)
```

To prepare the scene for the next section, where you will start scrolling the different layers in the game scene, you need to add another layer to your scene to hold all the sprites. You will do this by adding another SKSpriteNode named foregroundNode. This node will hold all the sprites that will affect game play. So let's add this node and add the player to it. First, add the following declaration of the foregroundNode immediately after the declaration of the backgroundNode:

```
let foregroundNode = SKSpriteNode()
```

© James Goodwill and Wesley Matlock 2017
J. Goodwill and W. Matlock, *Beginning Swift Games Development for iOS*,
DOI 10.1007/978-1-4842-2310-9_4

Next, add the foregroundNode instance to the scene by adding the following line of code immediately after where you added the backgroundNode to the scene:

```
addChild(foregroundNode)
```

Now find the location in the init() method where you added the playerNode and orbNode to the scene and change the addChild() invocations to the following:

```
foregroundNode.addChild(playerNode)
foregroundNode.addChild(orbNode)
```

Once you have the playerNode and orbNode added to the new foregroundNode, find where you are setting the position of the playerNode and change its position property using the following CGPoint:

```
playerNode.position = CGPoint(x: size.width / 2.0, y: 180.0)
```

Now find where you are setting the playerNode.physicsBody.dynamic property and turn off the player's dynamic volume.

```
playerNode.physicsBody?.isDynamic = false
```

You're doing this so the player doesn't fall off the screen if you don't tap the screen in time. Next, add the following new property to the GameScene immediately after the definition of the orbNode:

```
var impulseCount = 4
```

Now change the touchesBegan() method to match the following:

```
override func touchesBegan(_ touches: Set<UITouch>, with event: UIEvent?) {

    if !playerNode.physicsBody!.isDynamic {

        playerNode.physicsBody?.isDynamic = true
    }

    if impulseCount > 0 {

        playerNode.physicsBody!.applyImpulse(CGVector(dx: 0.0, dy: 40.0))
        impulseCount -= 1
    }
}
```

This snippet is turning the player's dynamic volume back on, if it was off, so the player will start reacting to gravity again. After that, it checks the impulseCount property. If it is greater than 0, then it applies an impulse to the player and decrements the impulseCount property by 1.

The purpose of this code is to put the game in an initial start state with the player stationary until you tap the screen to start. When the screen is tapped the first time, the game begins.

The `impulseCount` property was added to introduce a new game element. The game is going to use the `impulseCount` property to give the user a limited number of impulses that can be used for thrusts. The `impulseCount` property will increment each time the `playerNode` comes into contact with an orb and decrement every time the player taps the screen. This means the user must be good at collecting orbs, or they will eventually fall into oblivion and lose the game.

The next thing that needs to be changed is how the orb nodes are added to the scene. You want to add many more. Before adding additional nodes, the code that currently adds the nodes needs to be removed.

To remove this code, start by removing the `orbNode` property from the top of the `GameScene` class. Find the following line in the declarations section of the `GameScene` and remove it:

```
let orbNode = SKSpriteNode(imageNamed: "PowerUp")
```

Then remove all the following lines, which were used earlier to add the single node:

```
orbNode.position = CGPoint(x: 150.0, y: size.height - 25)
orbNode.physicsBody = SKPhysicsBody(circleOfRadius: orbNode.size.width / 2)
orbNode.physicsBody?.isDynamic = false
orbNode.physicsBody?.categoryBitMask = CollisionCategoryPowerUpOrbs
orbNode.physicsBody?.collisionBitMask = 0
orbNode.name = "POWER_UP_ORB"
foregroundNode.addChild(orbNode)
```

# Adding More Orbs to the Scene

The game scene is ready to start adding some real game components, the first of which is going to be a collection of additional orb nodes. These orbs will be laid out in two lines above the player. The first line of orbs, a collection of 20, will be centered and will start 100 points above the playNode, with 140 points in between each node's anchorPoint. The second set of orb nodes will also be a string of 20 nodes, but they will be 50 points to the right of the player. The code to add the first set of orb nodes is shown in the following snippet:

```
var orbNodePosition = CGPoint(x: playerNode.position.x, y: playerNode.position.y + 100)

for _ in 0...19 {

    let orbNode = SKSpriteNode(imageNamed: "PowerUp")

    orbNodePosition.y += 140
    orbNode.position = orbNodePosition
    orbNode.physicsBody = SKPhysicsBody(circleOfRadius: orbNode.size.width / 2)
    orbNode.physicsBody?.isDynamic = false

    orbNode.physicsBody?.categoryBitMask = CollisionCategoryPowerUpOrbs
    orbNode.physicsBody?.collisionBitMask = 0
    orbNode.name = "POWER_UP_ORB"

    foregroundNode.addChild(orbNode)

}
```

As you look over this code, you'll see a variable named orbNodePosition that has an x-coordinate matching the playerNode's x-coordinate and a y-coordinate that is 100 points above the playerNode.

After that there is a for loop that adds 20 orbNode objects centered above the player, with each node 140 points above the previous node's anchorPoint. Go ahead and add this code to the bottom of the GameScene's init() method, and then let's move on to the second set of orbNode objects.

To add the second set of nodes, you will use the following, similar code:

```
orbNodePosition = CGPoint(x: playerNode.position.x + 50, y: orbNodePosition.y)

for _ in 0...19 {

    let orbNode = SKSpriteNode(imageNamed: "PowerUp")

    orbNodePosition.y += 140
    orbNode.position = orbNodePosition
    orbNode.physicsBody = SKPhysicsBody(circleOfRadius: orbNode.size.width / 2)
    orbNode.physicsBody?.isDynamic = false

    orbNode.physicsBody?.categoryBitMask = CollisionCategoryPowerUpOrbs
    orbNode.physicsBody?.collisionBitMask = 0
    orbNode.name = "POWER_UP_ORB"

    foregroundNode.addChild(orbNode)
}
```

As you look over this code, you will see that the only change is the modification of the variable orbNodePosition. The value of the orbNodePosition's x-coordinate is increasing by 50, and everything else is the same. You could easily refactor this code into a method and pass it the new x-coordinate, but the goal here is to see how everything works. It will be refactored in a later chapter. Before moving on, go ahead and add this code after the previous loop in the GameScene's init() method.

After you have all this code added to the game scene, run the application. Your screen will now look like Figure 4-1.

*Figure 4-1. The modified scene with additional orbs*

The last thing you need to do before adding the scrolling to the game is change how orb contacts are handled. If you remember from Chapter 3, whenever the playerNode came into contact with an orbNode the orbNode was removed from the scene. This is still going to happen, but now the contact is going to also increment the impuleCount variable, giving the player additional impulses. To do this, change the current didBeginContact() method to the following:

```
func didBegin(_ contact: SKPhysicsContact) {

    let nodeB = contact.bodyB.node!

    if nodeB.name == "POWER_UP_ORB"  {

        impulseCount += 1
          nodeB.removeFromParent()
    }
}
```

The new didBeginContact() increases the impulseCount property each time the player comes into contact with an orb and then removes the orb. Now the player has additional fuel to keep from crashing into the planet's surface below.

To see this change in action, save your changes and run the game again. This time, when you tap the screen the player will be thrust upward and hit the first orb, then the second, and so on, until it flies off the top of the screen. If you tap long enough, the player will eventually run out of impulses and fall back through the bottom of the game.

# Scrolling the Scene

In this section you'll start adding movement to your game world. Before making any additional code changes, go back to Xcode and select the first background image in the Images.xcassets folder (Arrow 1), as shown in Figure 4-2. With the first background selected (Arrows 2 & 3), expand the Utilities section of Xcode (Arrow 4) and then click the Show Attributes Inspector button (Arrow 5). Notice the Image properties (Arrow 6). The height of the image is much greater than any of the currently available devices (Arrow 6).

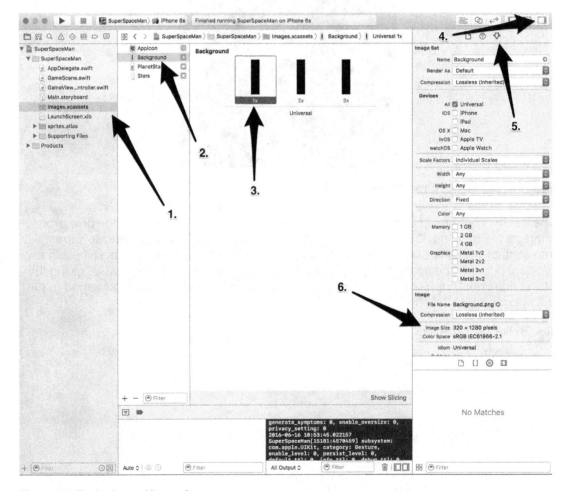

*Figure 4-2.* The background image size

The reason the background is so much bigger is because it's going to scroll downward to simulate the playerNode flying up through space. This is going to be accomplished by making use of the update() method in the game's rendering loop.

The first step to scroll the background is to change the position of the background based upon the location of the player in the game. Every time the player goes higher in the scene, the background will be moved down in the scene. The following code, which you will need to add to the GameScene in a moment, does just this:

```
override func update(_ currentTime: TimeInterval) {

    backgroundNode.position =
        CGPoint(x: backgroundNode.position.x,
                y: -((playerNode.position.y - 180.0)/8))
}
```

This implementation of the update() method changes the position of the background node based on the current position of the player. Specifically, it sets the position of the backgroundNode to its same x-value but uses a y-value that is 180 points below the position of the player, which is then divided by 8. Don't worry about these numbers at the moment. We'll talk about them a lot more in just a moment. Go ahead and add this update method to the end of the GameScene and then run the game again.

When you tap the screen this time, you will see the background slowly move toward the bottom of the scene as the player flies off the top of the screen. That's pretty cool, but the player is still flying out of the scene. There needs to be one more change made to the update() method. Take a look at this modified update():

```
override func update(_ currentTime: TimeInterval) {

    if playerNode.position.y >= 180.0 {

        backgroundNode.position =
            CGPoint(x: backgroundNode.position.x,
                    y: -((playerNode.position.y - 180.0)/8))

        foregroundNode.position =
            CGPoint(x: foregroundNode.position.x,
                    y: -(playerNode.position.y - 180.0))
    }
}
```

Notice two changes have been made. First, the method is checking to see whether the playerNode has moved at least 180 points up the scene. If the playerNode has moved this high, then the backgroundNode is moved down the scene at 1/8th the speed of the player, and the foreground is moved at exactly the same rate as the player. Moving the foreground at the same rate as the player prevents the player from going too high and leaving the scene. Change the current update() method to look like this one and run the application again.

When you tap the screen this time, the background moves slowly down the screen, and the SuperSpaceMan doesn't fly off the top of the screen. This is great except for one thing: when the playerNode gets to the top of the first line of orbs, the player can go no higher because the next set of orbs are to the right, and the player has no way of getting to them. This problem will be solved in the next section, when we show you how to add horizontal movement to the player using the accelerometer.

# Controlling Player Movement with the Accelerometer

In the previous section, the player ran into a problem when the next set of orbs needed to continue up the scene were 50 points to the right, but the player had no horizontal movement to reach them. You will now fix this problem by using the phone's accelerometer to control the player's movement along the x-axis.

To use the accelerometer in your game, you first need to add the CoreMotion framework to your GameScene. You do this by adding the following import statement to the top of your GameScene.swift file:

```
import CoreMotion
```

After this you need to add a new property. This property will hold an instance to the CMMotionManager object that will be used to monitor horizontal movement. Add this variable to the GameScene directly after the impulseCount variable added earlier:

```
let coreMotionManager = CMMotionManager()
```

That code creates an instance of the CMMotionManager and stores it in the constant coreMotionManager.

Let's talk a little about what CMMotionManager does. A CMMotionManager object is the object used to get access to the motion services provided by iOS. These services include access to the accelerometer, magnetometer, rotation rate, and other device motion sensors.

You are specifically interested in the acceleration along the x-axis of the device. This information is accessed using the accelerometer. You will be using the CMMotionManager to get the accelerometer to update the app on a specific interval with the current device acceleration. The code to do this is shown here:

```
coreMotionManager.accelerometerUpdateInterval = 0.3
coreMotionManager.startAccelerometerUpdates()
```

Take a moment to look at this code. The first line tells the coreMotionManager the interval, in seconds, that the accelerometer will use to update the app with the current acceleration. This value is set to 3/10ths of a second, which provides a pretty smooth update rate. You can play around with this value and see how it affects the app.

The second line of this code actually starts the accelerometer updates. Go ahead and add this code to the touchesBegan() method of the GameScene just after the playerNode.physicsBody.dynamic property is set to true. The modified touchesBegan() method is shown here:

```
override func touchesBegan(_ touches: Set<UITouch>, with event: UIEvent?) {

    if !playerNode.physicsBody!.isDynamic {

        playerNode.physicsBody?.isDynamic = true

        coreMotionManager.accelerometerUpdateInterval = 0.3
         coreMotionManager.startAccelerometerUpdates()
    }

    if impulseCount > 0 {

        playerNode.physicsBody!.applyImpulse(CGVector(dx: 0.0, dy: 40.0))
        impulseCount -= 1
    }
}
```

Now it's time to do something with this information. At first, using the update() method would seem like the logical location to put this data to use, but the update() method is invoked before the render loop has evaluated all the physics bodies in the scene. It's possible that colliding with another node in the scene could have altered the player's velocity along the x-axis, and this change should take place prior to altering the player's velocity with the accelerometer. Although that can't happen in this game—because the playerNode is the only dynamic volume in the game—it's good to be aware of.

Given that all the physics changes should be evaluated before the player's velocity on the x-axis is modified, there is really only one place in the render that can process accelerometer changes, and that is in the render loop's didSimulatePhysics() method. To override the current didSimulatePhysics(), add the following code to the bottom of the GameScene:

```
override func didSimulatePhysics() {

    if let accelerometerData = coreMotionManager.accelerometerData {

        playerNode.physicsBody!.velocity =
                CGVector(dx: CGFloat(accelerometerData.acceleration.x * 380.0),
                            dy: playerNode.physicsBody!.velocity.dy)
    }

    if playerNode.position.x < -(playerNode.size.width / 2) {

        playerNode.position =
            CGPoint(x: size.width - playerNode.size.width / 2,
                y: playerNode.position.y);
    }
    else if playerNode.position.x > self.size.width {
```

```
        playerNode.position = CGPoint(x: playerNode.size.width / 2,
                                      y: playerNode.position.y);
    }
}
```

Once you've added this code to the GameScene, save it and this time run the app on your physical iPhone. (The simulator doesn't simulate accelerometer activity.) When the app is running on your device, tap the screen and try to collect all the orbNodes. Remember, the more orbs you collect, the more impulses the player will have to keep going.

Once you've played around with the accelerometer a bit, let's look at the code you just added. The first line is where the playerNode's velocity is changed. This is done by creating a new vector with the most recent accelerometer x-acceleration value multiplied by 380.0 as the x-value, then using the player's current velocity along the y-axis, and finally making this the player's new overall velocity.

After the player's velocity is modified, there are two if statements to determine whether the player is flying off the scene either to the left or to the right. If either of these two conditions occurs, the player is moved to the opposite side of the scene. Notice when the location of the playerNode is tested, the test is checking to see whether half the playerNode is off the scene. This is done because the playerNode's anchor point is (0.5, 0.5).

There's one last change that needs to be made: turning off accelerometer updates when the GameScene is no longer used. To do that, add the following deinit() method to the bottom of the GameScene and save your changes:

```
deinit {

    coreMotionManager.stopAccelerometerUpdates()
}
```

# Summary

In this chapter you started to add some real functionality to your game. You began by making some small restructuring changes to the beginning of the game. Then you added additional orbNodes to collide with. After adding the new orbNodes, you added scrolling to your game scene, making it look like the player was flying through space collecting orbs. Finally, you closed out the chapter using the phone's accelerometer to move the player along the x-axis.

In the next chapter, you will continue adding new game elements as well as start animating your SKSpriteKitNodes. That is the chapter where you will start turning your game into a real, playable game.

# Chapter 5

# Adding Actions and Animations

In this chapter, you will refactor the orb node's layout one last time with the goal of enhancing playability. After that, we'll show you how you can use SKActions to move an SKSpriteNode back and forth across the scene and then make that same node rotate forever. We close out the chapter with a look at how you can add colorizing effects to an SKSpriteNode using a colorize action.

## Refactoring the Orb Node Layout One Last Time

Before we start talking about SKActions, a few changes need to be made to the way the orb nodes are laid out. Chapter 4 mentioned refactoring the layout of the orb nodes. In this section, we want to not only refactor the layout of the nodes into a method but also modify the layout of the orb nodes one last time. The goal of this modification is to lay out the orbs in a little more gamelike manner. This new method is shown here:

```
func addOrbsToForeground() {

    var orbNodePosition = CGPoint(x: playerNode.position.x, y: playerNode.position.y + 100)
    var orbXShift : CGFloat = -1.0

    for _ in 1...50 {

        let orbNode = SKSpriteNode(imageNamed: "PowerUp")

        if orbNodePosition.x - (orbNode.size.width * 2) <= 0 {

            orbXShift = 1.0
        }
```

```
    if orbNodePosition.x + orbNode.size.width >= size.width {

        orbXShift = -1.0
    }

    orbNodePosition.x += 40.0 * orbXShift
    orbNodePosition.y += 120
    orbNode.position = orbNodePosition
    orbNode.physicsBody = SKPhysicsBody(circleOfRadius: orbNode.size.width / 2)
    orbNode.physicsBody?.isDynamic = false

    orbNode.physicsBody?.categoryBitMask = CollisionCategoryPowerUpOrbs
    orbNode.physicsBody?.collisionBitMask = 0
    orbNode.name = "POWER_UP_ORB"

    foregroundNode.addChild(orbNode)
    }
}
```

As you look at this method, you'll see there's really nothing too special about it. It begins by setting the initial position of the first orb to be 100 points directly above the player node. It then adds 50 orbs, 40 points apart on the x-axis and 120 points apart on the y-axis, moving from right to left on the scene until all the nodes have been added. Go ahead and add this method to the GameScene directly after the init() method.

Once you have the addOrbsToForeground() method added to the game scene, then you need to add a call to invoke this method. Add the following method invocation to the end of the GameScene's init() method:

```
addOrbsToForeground()
```

Before invoking this new method, you need to remove the old orb-adding code from the init() method. To do so, find the following code and remove it from the init():

```
var orbNodePosition = CGPoint(x: playerNode.position.x, y: playerNode.position.y + 100)

for _ in 0...19 {

    let orbNode = SKSpriteNode(imageNamed: "PowerUp")

    orbNodePosition.y += 140
    orbNode.position = orbNodePosition
    orbNode.physicsBody = SKPhysicsBody(circleOfRadius: orbNode.size.width / 2)
    orbNode.physicsBody?.isDynamic = false

    orbNode.physicsBody?.categoryBitMask = CollisionCategoryPowerUpOrbs
    orbNode.physicsBody?.collisionBitMask = 0
    orbNode.name = "POWER_UP_ORB"

    foregroundNode.addChild(orbNode)
}
```

```
orbNodePosition = CGPoint(x: playerNode.position.x + 50, y: orbNodePosition.y)

for _ in 0...19 {

    let orbNode = SKSpriteNode(imageNamed: "PowerUp")

    orbNodePosition.y += 140
    orbNode.position = orbNodePosition
    orbNode.physicsBody = SKPhysicsBody(circleOfRadius: orbNode.size.width / 2)
    orbNode.physicsBody?.isDynamic = false

    orbNode.physicsBody?.categoryBitMask = CollisionCategoryPowerUpOrbs
    orbNode.physicsBody?.collisionBitMask = 0
    orbNode.name = "POWER_UP_ORB"

    foregroundNode.addChild(orbNode)
}
```

Once you've made and saved all these changes, run the app again and take a look at the new layout. It should look like Figure 5-1.

*Figure 5-1. The new orb layout*

After restarting the app, play around with the new layout. It's a lot more fun than just going straight up. You now have to fly side to side to collect orbs.

# Sprite Kit Actions

In Sprite Kit, whenever you want to move, modify, or perform some action on an SKNode, you're going to be, more often than not, applying that change using an SKAction. Apple defines an SKAction as follows: "An action is an object that defines a change you want to make to the scene." There are many different uses for SKActions, but some of the more common uses of SKActions are as follows:

> Animating a node through a series of textures
>
> Modifying the position of a node using its position property
>
> Changing the visibility of a node using its hidden property
>
> Adjusting the translucency of a node using its alpha property
>
> Modifying the size of a node using its size property
>
> Playing simple sounds
>
> Colorizing a node

To use an SKAction, you have to perform only two steps: you create the action you want to perform, and you tell the node you want to perform it on to run the action. Here's an example of this that moves a node to the right side of the scene over a period of two seconds:

```
var moveRightAction = SKAction.moveToX(size.width, duration: 2.0)
sampleNode.runAction(moveRightAction)
```

Another really cool feature of SKActions is the ability to chain actions together. Take a look at this example:

```
var moveRightAction = SKAction.moveToX(size.width, duration: 2.0)
var moveLeftAction = SKAction.moveToX(0.0, duration: 2.0)
var actionSequence = SKAction.sequence([moveRightAction, moveLeftAction])
sampleNode.runAction(actionSequence)
```

This bit of code will begin by moving the node to the right of the scene, and then when that action is finished, it will move the same node to the left side of the scene. Another nice feature of SKAction is the ability to repeat an action. Take a look at this snippet:

```
let moveLeftAction = SKAction.moveTo(x: 0.0, duration: 2.0)
let moveRightAction = SKAction.moveTo(x: size.width, duration: 2.0)
let actionSequence = SKAction.sequence([moveLeftAction, moveRightAction])
let moveAction = SKAction.repeatForever(actionSequence)
sampleNode.runAction(moveActionSequence)
```

Here you see the previous example, but now there is another action, repeatForever, that will run the moveAction forever. That's all it took—one line to make all the previous actions run forever.

Though this is a simple set of SKAction examples, there is almost no limit to how you can leverage actions in your games. In the following sections, we show you how to use some of this same code to move a collection of nodes back and forth across the scene while also rotating the node through a collection of textures, giving the illusion of node rotation.

> **Note**  Before moving on, take a look at all the methods used to create the SKActions. Note that all of these methods are class methods. This is the pattern used to create all SKActions. Currently there are no extensions of the SKAction class.

## Using Actions to Move Nodes in the Scene

In the previous section, we told you we were going to show you how to move a collection of nodes back and forth across the game scene. You've already seen how to do this using the moveToX, sequence, and repeatForever actions.

The node that will be moving across the scene is a new node. If you open the sprites. atlas folder, you'll see several BlackHoleX.png images. Select the first image in the list, BlackHole0.png. It should look like Figure 5-2.

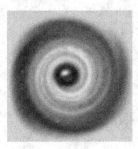

*Figure 5-2.  The BlackHole node*

The purpose of this node will be to represent a black hole moving back and forth across the scene. If the player node comes into contact with this node, the player will stop responding to the physics world and slowly fall to their death.

To add this new node to the scene, you need to create a new SKSpriteNode instance and pass it the BlackHole0 image. You can find the code to do this in the following method, named addBlackHolesToForeground():

```
func addBlackHolesToForeground() {

    let blackHoleNode = SKSpriteNode(imageNamed: "BlackHole0")
    blackHoleNode.position = CGPoint(x: size.width - 80.0, y: 600.0)
    blackHoleNode.physicsBody =
        SKPhysicsBody(circleOfRadius: blackHoleNode.size.width / 2)
    blackHoleNode.physicsBody?.isDynamic = false
    blackHoleNode.name = "BLACK_HOLE"

    foregroundNode.addChild(blackHoleNode)
}
```

You've seen all this code before. It starts by creating a new instance of the blackHoleNode using the image named BlackHole0. It then adds the node to the scene, sets the properties of the node's physicsBody, and names the node BLACK_HOLE. Go ahead and add this code immediately following the addOrbsToForeground() method. Then add a call to invoke the addBlackHolesToForeground() method right before the invocation of the addOrbsToForeground() method.

After you've made these changes, run the app again. This time you'll see the blackHoleNode suspended up and to the right of the player node, as shown in Figure 5-3.

*Figure 5-3. The BlackHole node added to the scene*

Before moving on to performing actions on this node, the code to handle contacts between the playerNode and the blackHoleNode needs to be added to the GameScene class. You've seen all this code before, so we'll go over it quickly without too much explanation.

First the categoryBitMask of the blackHoleNode needs to be configured, and the playNode's contactBitMask needs to be modified to include the blackHoleNode's categoryBitMask. To do this, add this definition of the CollisionCategoryBlackHoles constant directly below the other two category definitions, as shown here:

```
let CollisionCategoryPlayer : UInt32 = 0x1 << 1
let CollisionCategoryPowerUpOrbs : UInt32 = 0x1 << 2
let CollisionCategoryBlackHoles : UInt32 = 0x1 << 3
```

Next, set the blackHoleNode.physicsBody's categoryBitMask and collisionBitMask, as shown in the following snippet. Add these lines directly before the blackHoleNode is added to the foreground in the addBlackHolesToForeground() method:

```
blackHoleNode.physicsBody?.categoryBitMask = CollisionCategoryBlackHoles
blackHoleNode.physicsBody?.collisionBitMask = 0
```

After you've configured the blackHoleNode.physicsNody's bit masks, you need to add the CollisionCategoryBlackHoles to the playerNode.physicsBody's contactTestBitMask, as shown next. Find where the playerNode.physicsBody's contactTestBitMask is being set and modify it to look like this line:

```
playerNode.physicsBody?.contactTestBitMask =
    CollisionCategoryPowerUpOrbs | CollisionCategoryBlackHoles
```

You need to make one more change: modify the didBeginContact() method so that it tests for the BLACK_HOLE node whenever nodes come into contact with the playerNode. The simplest way to do this is to add an if else condition to the current if statement in the method. This change is shown in the following snippet:

```
if nodeB.name == "POWER_UP_ORB"  {

    impulseCount += 1
    nodeB.removeFromParent()
}
else if nodeB.name == "BLACK_HOLE"  {

    playerNode.physicsBody?.contactTestBitMask = 0
    impulseCount = 0
}
```

Make this change to the didBeginContact() method and run the app again. When you play this time, try to make the player come into contact with the new black hole. When you do, you'll notice the player quits responding to taps and contact with other nodes and then slowly falls until it falls through the bottom of the scene. At this point, the game is essentially over.

All right, it's finally time to use some SKActions. If you remember from the previous section, there are two steps involved when using an SKAction. First, you create the action you'd like to use, and then you tell the node that you want to apply the action to run the action. Let's begin with the action sequence used earlier in this chapter:

```
let moveLeftAction = SKAction.moveTo(x: 0.0, duration: 2.0)
let moveRightAction = SKAction.moveTo(x: size.width, duration: 2.0)
let actionSequence = SKAction.sequence([moveLeftAction, moveRightAction])
let moveAction = SKAction.repeatForever(actionSequence)
```

As you look at this code, you will recognize it from earlier in the chapter when we first introduced SKActions. The first line creates an action that will move the node that runs it to point 0.0 on the x-axis, and the second line moves the node back to the far-right side of the scene. After this, both of these actions are used to create a sequence of actions, and this new action is stored in the variable actionSequence. Finally, the actionSequence is used to create a repeating action using the SKAction.repeatForever() class method. After you've looked this code over a bit, copy it to the top of the addBlackHolesToForeground() method.

The final step to make the black hole move back and forth across the scene is to tell the blackHoleNode to actually run the action. You do that using the following single line:

```
blackHoleNode.run(moveAction)
```

Add this line to the end of the addBlackHolesToForeground() method and run the app again. This time you'll see the black hole moving back and forth across the scene for as long as the game is being run.

There is one more thing we want to do with the addBlackHolesToForeground() method before moving on. You may have noticed the name of the addBlackHolesToForeground() method mentions more than one black hole. This was intentional. We think the game needs several black holes to make it more difficult to play. Take a look at the new addBlackHolesToForeground() method shown here:

```
func addBlackHolesToForeground() {

    let moveLeftAction = SKAction.moveTo(x: 0.0, duration: 2.0)
    let moveRightAction = SKAction.moveTo(x: size.width, duration: 2.0)
    let actionSequence = SKAction.sequence([moveLeftAction, moveRightAction])
    let moveAction = SKAction.repeatForever(actionSequence)

    for i in 1...10 {

        let blackHoleNode = SKSpriteNode(imageNamed: "BlackHole0")

        blackHoleNode.position = CGPoint(x: size.width - 80.0, y: 600.0 * CGFloat(i))
        blackHoleNode.physicsBody = SKPhysicsBody(circleOfRadius: blackHoleNode.size.width / 2)
        blackHoleNode.physicsBody?.isDynamic = false
        blackHoleNode.physicsBody?.categoryBitMask = CollisionCategoryBlackHoles
        blackHoleNode.physicsBody?.collisionBitMask = 0
        blackHoleNode.name = "BLACK_HOLE"

        blackHoleNode.run(moveAction)
        blackHoleNode.run(rotateAction)

        foregroundNode.addChild(blackHoleNode)
    }
}
```

Note that this code iterates over a for loop 10 times, adding another black hole every 600 points above the previous black hole. As it does so, it tells each new node to run the moveAction created earlier. To see this change in action, use this code to replace the current addBlackHolesToForeground() method and run the app. When you run the app this time, you will see additional black holes going up the length of the scene.

# Using SKActions to Animate Sprites

This section shows you how to leverage SKActions to animate the black hole nodes that you just added to the scene. In doing so, it introduces you to a couple of new classes: SKTexture and SKTextureAtlas.

An SKTexture is an object that holds an image that is used by SKSpriteNodes, SKShapeNodes, or as the particles created by an SKEmitterNode. You've been using SKTexture throughout this book when you've created an SKSpriteNode. Each image used to create an SKSpriteNode is internally represented as an SKTexture.

An SKTextureAtlas is a collection of SKTexture objects created from a texture atlas stored in an application's resource bundle. Go back to your project in Xcode and open the folder named sprites.atlas. You'll see all the images, except background images, used in this game. If you wanted to load all of the images in this atlas folder into an SKTextureAtlas, you would execute the following code:

```
let textureAtlas = SKTextureAtlas(named: "sprites.atlas")
```

This single line reads all the individual files in the sprites.atlas folder and adds them to the SKTextureAtlas, each as an SKTexture that can be looked up by the original file name. Add this line to the top of the addBlackHolesToForeground() method, and let's move on.

To retrieve an SKTexture, you would use the SKTextureAtlas.textureNamed() method, passing it the name of the texture you want to retrieve. Here's an example of this that retrieves the first black hole texture in the textureAtlas:

```
let frame0 = textureAtlas.textureNamed("BlackHole0")
```

This line of code retrieves the SKTexture represented by the name BlackHole0 and stores it in the constant frame0.

To create an animation using all the black hole images, you would retrieve each of them from the textureAtlas and add them to an array that represents the order each texture will be displayed in the animation. This code is shown in the following snippet:

```
let frame0 = textureAtlas.textureNamed("BlackHole0")
let frame1 = textureAtlas.textureNamed("BlackHole1")
let frame2 = textureAtlas.textureNamed("BlackHole2")
let frame3 = textureAtlas.textureNamed("BlackHole3")
let frame4 = textureAtlas.textureNamed("BlackHole4")

let blackHoleTextures = [frame0, frame1, frame2, frame3, frame4]
```

Once you've examined this code, add it to the top of the addBlackHolesToForeground() method immediately after the creation of the textureAtlas.

Now, all you have to do to animate the black holes is create a new action using the SKAction.animate() method, passing it the array of textures and the time, in seconds, that each frame is to be displayed. Take a look at the following lines:

```
let animateAction = SKAction.animate(with: blackHoleTextures, timePerFrame: 0.2)
let rotateAction = SKAction.repeatForever(animateAction)
```

The first line creates an action that will display each texture in the textureAtlas array for 2/10ths of a second. To make the black hole nodes animate forever, the second line creates another action that will perform the animation action forever. To see your new animation in action, copy all this code to the top of the addBlackHolesToForeground() method immediately after the blackHoleTextures array and then add the following line, which will run the action, right before you add each blackHoleNode to the scene:

```
blackHoleNode.runAction(rotateAction)
```

When you've made all of these changes to the addBlackHolesToForeground() method, the new method will look like the following:

```
func addBlackHolesToForeground() {

    let textureAtlas = SKTextureAtlas(named: "sprites.atlas")

    let frame0 = textureAtlas.textureNamed("BlackHole0")
    let frame1 = textureAtlas.textureNamed("BlackHole1")
    let frame2 = textureAtlas.textureNamed("BlackHole2")
    let frame3 = textureAtlas.textureNamed("BlackHole3")
    let frame4 = textureAtlas.textureNamed("BlackHole4")

    let blackHoleTextures = [frame0, frame1, frame2, frame3, frame4]

    let animateAction = SKAction.animate(with: blackHoleTextures, timePerFrame: 0.2)
    let rotateAction = SKAction.repeatForever(animateAction)

    let moveLeftAction = SKAction.moveTo(x: 0.0, duration: 2.0)
    let moveRightAction = SKAction.moveTo(x: size.width, duration: 2.0)
    let actionSequence = SKAction.sequence([moveLeftAction, moveRightAction])
    let moveAction = SKAction.repeatForever(actionSequence)

    for i in 1...10 {

        let blackHoleNode = SKSpriteNode(imageNamed: "BlackHole0")

        blackHoleNode.position = CGPoint(x: size.width - 80.0, y: 600.0 * CGFloat(i))
        blackHoleNode.physicsBody = SKPhysicsBody(circleOfRadius: blackHoleNode.size.width / 2)
        blackHoleNode.physicsBody?.isDynamic = false
        blackHoleNode.physicsBody?.categoryBitMask = CollisionCategoryBlackHoles
        blackHoleNode.physicsBody?.collisionBitMask = 0
        blackHoleNode.name = "BLACK_HOLE"

        blackHoleNode.run(moveAction)
        blackHoleNode.run(rotateAction)

        foregroundNode.addChild(blackHoleNode)
    }
}
```

Once you've made all these changes, save your work and run the application again. This time you'll see that as the black holes are moving back and forth across the scene, they're also rotating as they are animated through each of the textures in the `blackHoleTextures` array.

# Adding Some Additional Bling to the GameScene

Now that you have all the orbs laid out nicely and the black holes are animating back and forth across the game scene, it's time to add a little more bling to make the game scene look just a little better. Specifically, we show how to add some additional stars to the scene, a planet surface, and how to colorize the `playerNode` when it comes into contact with a black hole.

Let's get started with adding some stars to the background. First, open the `Images.xcassets` folder in Xcode and select the image `Stars`. To add this image to the scene, first add a declaration statement that will hold the reference to the `SKSpriteNode` referencing the `Stars` image. This declaration should be added to the `GameScene` directly after the `backgroundNode` declaration:

```
let backgroundNode = SKSpriteNode(imageNamed: "Background")
let backgroundStarsNode = SKSpriteNode(imageNamed: "Stars")
```

After adding the declaration, add the following lines to the `GameScene.init(size: CGSize)` method immediately after the line that adds the `backgroundNode` to the scene:

```
addChild(backgroundNode)
backgroundStarsNode.size.width = frame.size.width
backgroundStarsNode.anchorPoint = CGPoint(x: 0.5, y: 0.0)
backgroundStarsNode.position = CGPoint(x: 160.0, y: 0.0)
addChild(backgroundStarsNode)
```

You need to do one last thing before running the app and checking out the new stars: move the stars in relation to the `playerNode`. Moving the stars in relation to the player is pretty straightforward, but we do want to add a little coolness by moving the stars at a slightly different rate than the background. We have modified the `update()` method to do just this. Take a look:

```
override func update(_ currentTime: TimeInterval) {

    if playerNode.position.y >= 180.0 {

        backgroundNode.position = CGPoint(x: backgroundNode.position.x, y:
            -((playerNode.position.y - 180.0)/8));

            backgroundStarsNode.position = CGPoint(x: backgroundStarsNode.position.x, y:
                -((playerNode.position.y - 180.0)/6))

        foregroundNode.position = CGPoint (x: foregroundNode.position.x, y:
            -(playerNode.position.y - 180.0));
    }
}
```

Notice the bolded section of the modified update() method there. With these two lines we're moving the stars relative to the playerNode, but we're moving them at a slightly slower rate than the backgroundNode. This gives the illusion that the backgroundStarsNode is closer to the viewport of the scene. Make this change to the update() method and run the application again. When the game is first launched, you'll see a scene that looks like Figure 5-4.

*Figure 5-4. A layer of stars added to the scene*

Go ahead and start playing the game. When you go higher and higher in the scene, you'll notice that the stars are moving just a bit faster than the background. This effect is called *parallaxation*.

The next thing you want to do is add the perception that the playerNode is starting on a planet's surface. Go back to Xcode, open the Images.xcassets folder once again, and find the PlanetStart image. This is the image that will act as the planet's surface.

Adding this new image to your scene isn't complicated, and you've seen it before. The only difference from adding the stars to the scene is that you're going to move the planet at the same rate as the background node. This will make the planet's surface fall away as the player gets higher and higher in the scene.

Let's go ahead and do this. First, add a new SKSpriteNode declaration directly following the declaration of the backgroundStarsNode:

```
let backgroundStarsNode = SKSpriteNode(imageNamed: "Stars")
let backgroundPlanetNode = SKSpriteNode(imageNamed: "PlanetStart")
```

Next, insert the code to add the backgroundPlanetNode to the scene. This code should immediately follow the addition of the backgroundStarsNode, as shown here:

```
addChild(backgroundStarsNode)

backgroundPlanetNode.size.width = frame.size.width
backgroundPlanetNode.anchorPoint = CGPoint(x: 0.5, y: 0.0)
backgroundPlanetNode.position = CGPoint(x: size.width / 2.0, y: 0.0)
addChild(backgroundPlanetNode)
```

Now, find the line of code that sets the position of the playerNode (in the init(size: CGSize) method) and change the position to match the following:

```
playerNode.position = CGPoint(x: size.width / 2.0, y: 220.0)
```

Finally, modify the update method to move the backgroundPlanetNode at the same rate as the backgroundNode.

```
override func update(_ currentTime: TimeInterval) {

    if playerNode.position.y >= 180.0 {

        backgroundNode.position = CGPoint(x: backgroundNode.position.x, y: -((playerNode.
        position.y - 180.0)/8));
        backgroundStarsNode.position = CGPoint(x: backgroundStarsNode.position.x, y:
        -((playerNode.position.y - 180.0)/6));
        backgroundPlanetNode.position = CGPoint(x: backgroundPlanetNode.position.x, y:
        -((playerNode.position.y - 180.0)/8));
        foregroundNode.position = CGPoint(x: foregroundNode.position.x, y: -(playerNode.
        position.y - 180.0));
    }
}
```

Once you've made all these changes, run the app again and admire your handiwork. You should now see a planet resting at the bottom of the scene and the playerNode standing on top of it. Tap the screen a few times. The planet and the background will move together, giving the impression that the playerNode is flying off the planet's surface and into space. Figure 5-5 shows the new scene.

*Figure 5-5.  A planet's surface added to the scene*

There's one last change we would like to make. If you've had the player run into a black hole recently, you'll know that it's a bit anticlimactic. We want to add a visual indicator that shows the player is dead. A simple way to do this is to use a colorize action. A colorize action will blend a second color into an SKNode over a specified interval. Here's an example creation of colorizeAction:

```
SKAction.colorize(with: UIColor.red(), colorBlendFactor: 0.5, duration: 1)
```

This action, when run on an SKNode, will blend a red color with a blend factor of 0.5 over a period of 1 second. This is similar to what we would like to apply to the playerNode when it comes into contact with a black hole. Take a look at the last two lines of this modified didBeginContact's method:

```
extension GameScene: SKPhysicsContactDelegate {

    func didBegin(_ contact: SKPhysicsContact) {

        let nodeB = contact.bodyB.node!

        if nodeB.name == "POWER_UP_ORB"  {
```

```
        impulseCount += 1
        nodeB.removeFromParent()
    }
    else if nodeB.name == "BLACK_HOLE"  {

        playerNode.physicsBody?.contactTestBitMask = 0
        impulseCount = 0

        let colorizeAction = SKAction.colorize(with: UIColor.red, colorBlendFactor: 1.0,
        duration: 1)
        playerNode.run(colorizeAction)
    }
  }
}
```

These two lines create a colorize action that will fully blend a red color to the playerNode over a period of one second whenever the player runs into a black hole. Make these changes and run the application one more time. When you run it this time, be sure to run the player into a black hole. Notice how, when he does, he will slowly turn red and fall to the planet's surface—much better.

# Summary

In this chapter, you refactored the orb node's layout one last time with the goal of enhancing playability. After that, you saw how to use SKActions to move an SKSpriteNode back and forth across the scene and then make that same node rotate forever. At the end of the chapter, you took a look at how you can add colorizing effects to an SKSpriteNode using a colorize action.

In the next chapter, we focus on using particle emitters and how they can be leveraged in Sprite Kit games. After that, we show you how they can be used to add engine exhaust to the playerNode whenever an impulse is applied to the physicsBody.

# Chapter 6

# Adding Particle Effects to Your Game with Emitter Nodes

In this chapter, we show you how to define particle emitters and how to leverage them in SpriteKit games. After that, we show you how you can use them to add engine exhaust to the playerNode whenever an impulse is applied to the physicsBody.

> **Note** We cover only the properties that we'll be using in the SuperSpaceMan game. If you want to see the complete list of properties, check out the Apple Developer docs at https://developer. apple.com/library/ios/documentation/SpriteKit/Reference/SKEmitterNode_Ref/ index.html and https://developer.apple.com/library/ios/documentation/IDEs/ Conceptual/xcode_guide-particle_emitter/Introduction/Introduction.html.

Particle emitters are a really cool and easy-to-use feature provided by SpriteKit. You can use them to create special effects that simulate anything from fire to rain. SpriteKit implements these effects using the class SKEmitterNode.

An SKEmitterNode object is a node that creates and renders small particle sprites. These sprites are owned by SpriteKit and are not directly accessible by your game. You can't modify the individual sprites yourself, but you can modify the properties of the SKEmitterNode instance.

© James Goodwill and Wesley Matlock 2017
J. Goodwill and W. Matlock, *Beginning Swift Games Development for iOS*,
DOI 10.1007/978-1-4842-2310-9_6

You can create particle emitters by hand, but it's much easier to create a particle emitter using Xcode's built-in Particle Emitter Editor. The Particle Emitter Editor is a graphical editor built into Xcode that provides a visual environment in which you can design custom particle effects. Figure 6-1 shows Xcode's Particle Emitter Editor.

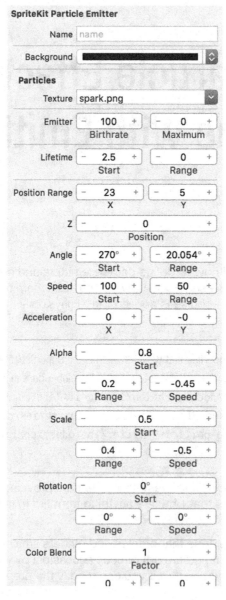

*Figure 6-1. Xcode's Particle Emitter Editor*

# Using Particle Emitter Templates

In addition to being able to create custom effects, the Particle Emitter Editor offers a collection of prebuilt particle templates. These templates give you a great starting point for creating your own custom effects. Table 6-1 describes each of these templates.

*Table 6-1. Xcode's Prepackaged Particle Emitter Templates*

| Template Name | Use |
| --- | --- |
| Bokeh | This template creates a hexagonal collection of particles that grow and blur and then fade out at the end of their life cycles. |
| Fire | This template creates a fire effect that you might use as a torch or, just maybe, as the exhaust of a spaceman. |
| Fireflies | The Fireflies template creates a collection of yellow particles that randomly move a short distance while growing and blurring and then fading out at the end of their life cycles. |
| Magic | The Magic template creates a collection of green (by default) particles that also randomly move a short distance while growing and blurring before fading out at the end of their life cycles. |
| Rain | The Rain template does just what you would think it would: it creates a collection of particles that start at the top of the emitter and move toward the bottom of the screen with the purpose of emulating a rain storm. |
| Smoke | The Smoke template creates several large black particles that start at the bottom of the emitter and move toward the top of the screen. As each particle moves toward the top of the screen, it slowly fades out. |
| Snow | The Snow template creates white, diffuse, round particles that start at the top of the emitter and, like the Rain particles, move toward the bottom of the screen. |
| Spark | The Spark template creates short-lived, golden particles that burst out of the emitter in all 360 degrees before fading out to nothing. |

# Creating a Particle Emitter

Let's start playing around with these particle emitters. In Xcode, create a new iOS project, using the Game template. Name it whatever you like and save the project wherever you like. This project will be a "throwaway" project used only as a play area for your emitter experiments.

Once you have the project created, click File ➤ New and choose SpriteKit Particle File template from the iOS ➤ Resource category, as shown in Figure 6-2.

*Figure 6-2. The Choose Template dialog*

Now click the Next button and select the Spark particle template, as shown in Figure 6-3.

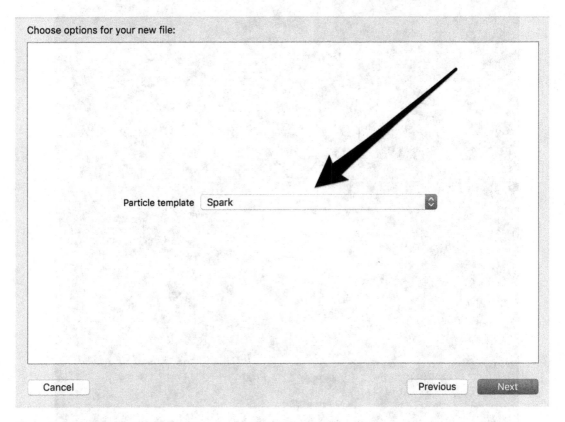

*Figure 6-3. The Choose File Options dialog*

After making sure you have the correct particle template selected, click Next again and name the file MySparkParticle. Next, select the MySparkParticle.sks file. This time you'll see an image similar to Figure 6-4.

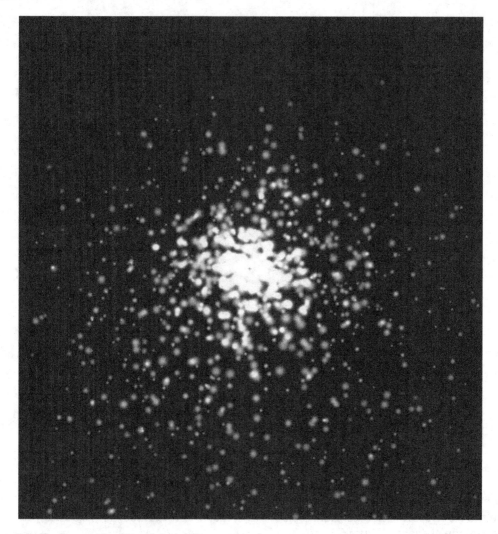

*Figure 6-4.* *The generated spark particle emitter*

What you're seeing here is a collection of many versions of the white smudge image, each representing a single particle generated by this particle emitter. The reason each particle looks so different from the spark.png file is because the emitter is modifying each particle image according to the emitter's property settings.

# Particle Emitter Properties

To see how these properties are being set, with the MySparkParticle.sks file selected, open the Utilities pane on the right side of Xcode and click the Show the SKNode inspector button. This will show each of the properties of the current particle emitter. You can see these attributes in Figure 6-5.

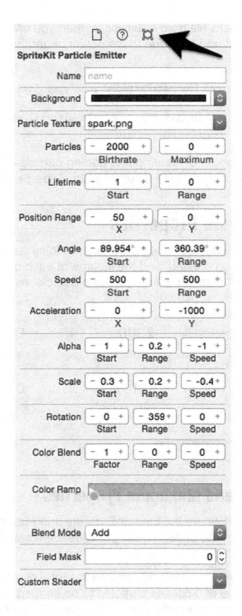

*Figure 6-5.* *The SpriteKit particle emitter properties*

Each of the properties in this Particle Emitter Editor changes the way each of the particles is emitted. Once you've modified each of the emitter properties you're interested in, Xcode saves the emitter properties in a SpriteKit particle file with the .sks extension. The resulting file contains an archived SKEmitterNode object configured to run the particle effects designed in the editor. When you want to use the particle emitter in your game, you first get the path to the `.sks` file from `mainBundle`; then you use this path to unarchive the `SKEmitterNode` object and add the node to the scene or another `SKNode`:

```
let pathToEmitter =
    Bundle.main.path(forResource: "MySparkParticle", ofType: "sks")
let emitter =
    NSKeyedUnarchiver.unarchiveObject(withFile: pathToEmitter!) as? SKEmitterNode
addChild(emitter!)
```

This is the most common process of creating and adding particle emitters to your game. Let's take a look at the properties that will be used in the SuperSpaceMan game.

# The Particle Life-Cycle Properties

The particle life-cycle properties determine how many particles are created, the maximum number of particles that can be created, and the lifetime of each of the created particles. There are four properties that control the life cycle of a particle, as shown in Figure 6-6.

**Figure 6-6.** *The SpriteKit particle life-cycle properties*

## The Emitter Birthrate and Maximum Properties

The first two life-cycle properties are the Emitter Birthrate and Maximum properties. The Birthrate property defines the rate at which new particles are emitted per second. The higher the value, the faster new particles are generated.

The Maximum particle life-cycle property determines the total number of particles to be emitted by the emitter. A value of 0 causes particles to be emitted indefinitely. Any other value will cause the emitter to stop emitting when that value is reached.

To see how these two properties work together, go back to the SpriteKit Particle Emitter properties editor in Xcode and change the Birthrate property to 20 and the Maximum property to 0. Watch what happens—the emitter generates 20 particles per second.

Now leave the Birthrate property at 20, change the Maximum property to 20, and check out how the emitter changes. This time the emitter will emit 20 particles over 1 second and then stop for 1 second and then emit another 20 particles. It will repeat this process forever. When you have finished playing around with these two properties, change the Birthrate property back to 2000 and the Maximum property back to 0.

# The Lifetime Start and Range Properties

The next two particle life-cycle properties are the Start and Range properties. These properties control the lifetime of the emitted particles. The Start property controls the average length of time in seconds that a particle is visible. When the time elapses, the particle fades away.

The Range property provides a method of varying the time a particle is on the screen. When you set this property to any number other than 0, then a random number between 0 and the entered number is generated. Half of that number is then randomly added or subtracted to the Start value to produce the final lifetime of the particle. If you enter 0, then all particles will stay visible for the same amount of time.

# The Particle Movement Properties

There are five sets of properties that affect the movement of particles being emitted, as shown in Figure 6-7 and described in the following sections.

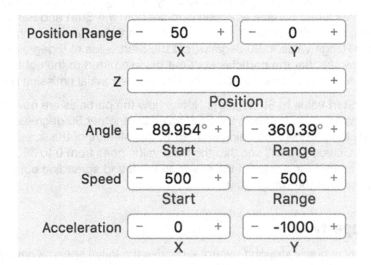

*Figure 6-7. The SpriteKit particle movement properties*

## The Position Range Property

The Position Range property defines the area in which the emitted particles are created. The particles are created within a rectangle defined by the Position Range property's X and Y values.

To see how this works, go back to the MySparkParticle.sks file and change the Position Range property's X value to 300 and the Y value to 300 and watch how this affects the emission of the particles. You will now see the particles being emitted in a 300×300 box. Play around with these properties until you are comfortable with how they work.

## The Z-position Property

The Z-position property controls the particle's average starting depth along the z-axis. You can think of this property as controlling how near or far the particle will be placed from the viewport.

## The Angle Property

The next particle movement property is the Angle property. The Angle property defines the angle at which particles travel away from the creation point in counterclockwise degrees. There are two Angle values: Start and Range.

The Start value defines the direction, in degrees, that a particle is emitted, and the Range value defines the number of degrees, plus or minus half of the number value, that the particle's initial angle varies. This all sounds complicated, so let's play around with these values and see what happens.

If you look at the initial value of the spark emitter's Angle property, you'll see that it's roughly 90 degrees, and the Range property is set to roughly 360 degrees. The easiest way to see how these values affect particle emission is to set both the Start and Range values. Currently, Range is set to 360 degrees, which says the particle emission range is a complete circle. Reduce the Range value to 90 degrees, set the Start value to 0 degrees, and see what happens. You'll now see that the particles start out being emitted to the right of the screen and spread out to roughly 45 degrees above and below their initial emission point.

Now increase the Start value to 90 degrees. Notice how the particles are now beginning their life being emitted straight up. Increase the Start value by another 90 degrees, making it 180 degrees. This time the particles are being emitted to the left side of the screen. After playing around with these values, you will see that the Start value goes from 0 to 360 degrees counterclockwise around the center of the emission point and spreading out from the Start value by half the value of the Range value.

## The Speed Property

The Speed property is pretty straightforward. It defines the initial speed a particle moves at creation. You specify the initial speed using the Start value, and then you can use the Range value to adjust the initial speed for a particle, plus or minus half the Range value. Setting the Range value to 0 means that all particles travel at the same speed.

## The Acceleration Property

The final particle movement property is the Acceleration property. The Acceleration property controls the degree to which a particle accelerates or decelerates after emission in terms of both X and Y directions. You use the X value to apply acceleration along the x-axis and use the Y value to apply acceleration along the y-axis.

It's common to use the Acceleration property to simulate a gravity effect. The easiest way to see how this works is to change all the emitter properties so they match the values in Figure 6-8.

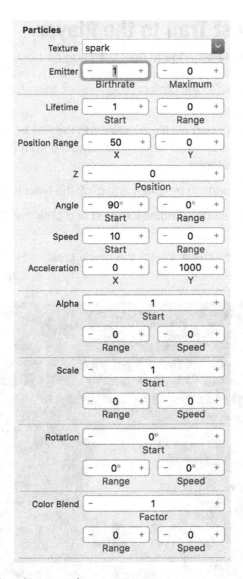

*Figure 6-8. The modified particle emitter properties*

If you don't see a property in this figure, then you don't have to worry about changing it. After you've made these changes, you'll see a single particle moving straight up along the y-axis. The reason the particle is going straight up is because all of the acceleration is along the y-axis.

Change the X value for the Acceleration property to 500 and see what happens. The particle now moves up the y-axis and to the right along the x-axis. Next, change the X value for the Acceleration property to –500. You'll now see that the particle is again moving up along the y-axis, but this time it's moving left along the x-axis. That's because you applied a negative X acceleration.

# Adding an Exhaust Trail to the Player

It's now time to put this new knowledge to use. Let's add an exhaust trail to the playerNode using a particle emitter. To do that, you need to switch back to the SuperSpaceMan project and add a new particle emitter to the project. You've seen this process previously, but here are the abbreviated steps:

1.  Add a new SpriteKit particle file by selecting the File ➤ New File Menu and choose SpriteKit Particle File template from the iOS ➤ Resource category.

2.  Select Fire as the particle template and click the Next button.

3.  Name the particle emitter **EngineExhaust** and click the Create button.

Once you've completed these steps, select the newly created EngineExhaust.sks file. You'll see an image similar to Figure 6-9.

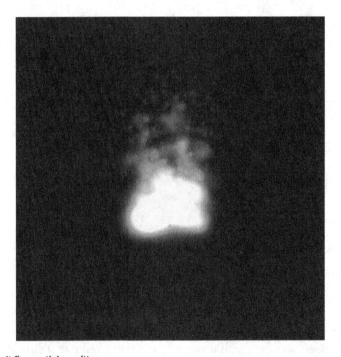

*Figure 6-9. The default fire particle emitter*

This looks really good, but to emulate exhaust emitting from the spaceman as he flies up the scene, the angle of the emitting fire needs to be rotated by 180 degrees. To make this happen, change the Start value for the Angle property to 270 degrees, and to resize the emitted flame's width, reduce the Position Range's X value to 23. Figure 6-10 shows these changes.

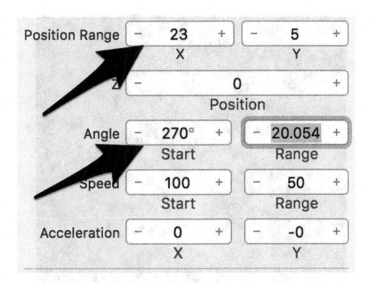

*Figure 6-10. The inverted fire particle emitter property changes*

Once you've made these changes, you'll see that the fire is now being emitted toward the bottom of the screen, and the width of the flame has been reduced. This looks much better, but we think it would look even better if the flames were a little subtler. The easiest way to make this happen is to reduce the Birthrate value of the particles being emitted. Do that by reducing the particle Birthrate value to 100, as shown in Figure 6-11.

*Figure 6-11. The reduced particle Birthrate value changes*

Awesome. Save your changes, and let's take a look at the new particle emitter shown in Figure 6-12.

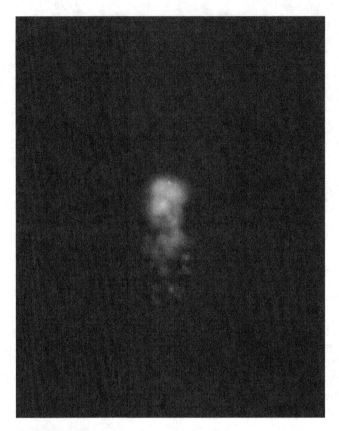

*Figure 6-12. The final particle emitter*

This is exactly what was needed. The fire is being emitted in the correct direction, and the size and Birthrate values will fit nicely attached to the playerNode.

Let's start using the new emitter. If you remember from the previous sections, once you have the emitter looking like you want it to, it's really easy to add to your scene. The first thing you need to do is load the SKEmitterNode using your new SKS file. This is pretty simple and can be accomplished by first adding a new SKEmitterNode named engineExhaust right before the first GameScene.init() method. This declaration is shown here:

```
var engineExhaust: SKEmitterNode?
```

After you make this change, add the following lines of code to the bottom of the second GameScene.init() method:

```
let engineExhaustPath = Bundle.main.path(forResource: "EngineExhaust", ofType: "sks")
engineExhaust = NSKeyedUnarchiver.unarchiveObject(withFile: engineExhaustPath!) as?
SKEmitterNode
engineExhaust?.position = CGPoint(x: 0.0, y: -(playerNode.size.height / 2))
```

You've seen these lines before, with the exception of the last line. That line sets the position of the emitter to a point at (0.0, -(self.playerNode.size.height / 2)). We're using this point because the emitter will need to be added to the playerNode, and the playerNode's anchor point is the middle of the player. Using the negative value of half the size of the playerNode will place the emitter at the bottom of the playerNode.

OK, so far you have the emitter node loaded, and you're ready to add it the playerNode. You can do that with the following two lines:

```
playerNode.addChild(engineExhaust!)
engineExhaust?.isHidden = true
```

As you look over this change, you'll see that the code is pretty straightforward. First the engineExhaust emitter node is added to the playerNode, and then the exhaust is hidden. We're hiding the exhaust here because we want the exhaust emitter to be visible only when the player of the game taps the screen. Add this code right after the line that sets the position of the engineExhaust node.

There's one more thing you need to do, which is make the engineExhaust visible when the user taps the screen. To do that, add the following line of code to the end of the second if statement in the touchesBegan() method and run the game again:

```
engineExhaust?.isHidden = false
```

Notice that when you tap the screen this time, not only does the spaceman fly up through the scene, this time there's an exhaust stream coming out of the bottom of the playerNode.

This looks great, but there's one problem. Even when you're no longer tapping the screen, the exhaust emitter is still visible. The emitter should be removed after a moment so that it emulates a quick burst of force that goes away after a short period of time. This problem can be fixed easily enough with an NSTimer.

To fix this problem, you need to modify the touchesBegan() method to start a timer each time the screen is tapped and an impulse is applied. The modified if statement is shown here:

```
if impulseCount > 0 {

    playerNode.physicsBody?.applyImpulse(CGVector(dx: 0.0, dy: 40.0))
    impulseCount -= 1

    engineExhaust?.isHidden = false

    Timer.scheduledTimer(timeInterval: 0.5,
        target: self,
        selector: #selector(GameScene.hideEngineExaust(_:)),
        userInfo: nil,
        repeats: false)
}
```

As you look over these changes, you'll notice that at the end of the if statement a new timer is created that will run the hideEngineExhaust() method half a second after the timer is scheduled. The hideEngineExhaust() method that will be invoked is shown here:

```
func hideEngineExaust(_ timer:Timer!) {

    if !engineExhaust!.isHidden {
```

```
            engineExhaust?.isHidden = true
    }
}
```

Examining the hideEngineExhaust() method, you'll see that it does exactly what it sounds like it will do. It first checks to see whether the engineExhaust is visible and hides it if it is.

Make these changes to the touchesBegan() method and add the hideEngineExhaust() method to the bottom of the GameScene. Once you've made these changes, run the app again. This time you'll notice the exhaust is added to the playerNode each time you tap the screen and will be removed from the playerNode half a second after the last tap. This looks much better. Before closing out this chapter, make sure the final touchesBegan() method looks like the following:

```
override func touchesBegan(_ touches: Set<UITouch>, with event: UIEvent?) {

    if !playerNode.physicsBody!.isDynamic {

        playerNode.physicsBody?.isDynamic = true

        coreMotionManager.accelerometerUpdateInterval = 0.3
        coreMotionManager.startAccelerometerUpdates()
    }

    if impulseCount > 0 {

        playerNode.physicsBody?.applyImpulse(CGVector(dx: 0.0, dy: 40.0))
        impulseCount -= 1

        engineExhaust!.isHidden = false

    Timer.scheduledTimer(timeInterval: 0.5,
        target: self,
        selector: #selector(GameScene.hideEngineExaust(_:)),
        userInfo: nil,
        repeats: false)
    }
}
```

# Summary

In this chapter, we briefly introduced you to particle emitters, including taking a quick look at some of Xcode's template emitters. After that, we showed you how to add a particle emitter to the playerNode so that you can emulate engine exhaust whenever an impulse is applied to the physicsBody.

In Chapter 7, you'll get your first look at SpriteKit's SKTextNode when we show you how to add scoring to the SuperSpaceMan game. After that, you'll get a look at another use for SKAction when you add sound to the SuperSpaceMan game.

# Adding Points and Sound

In this chapter, we talk about using SKLabelNodes to add labels to your SpriteKit games. Specifically, we show you how to add a label that keeps up with the number of impulses remaining for the SuperSpaceMan to use, and then we show you how to add scoring to the game to keep up with the number of orbs the SuperSpaceMan has collected.

At the end of the chapter, you'll get a chance to revisit SKActions when we show you how to use them to add simple game sounds.

## Introducing SKLabelNodes

As mentioned, SpriteKit implements text labels using a class named SKLabelNode. The SKLabelNode class, just like all the nodes you've seen so far, is an extension of SKNode. It's a pretty simple class with only two init() methods and a handful of properties, all focused on setting label fonts, colors, and layout.

The simplest way to use an SKLabelNode is shown in the following snippet:

```
let simpleLabel = SKLabelNode(fontNamed: "Copperplate")
simpleLabel.text = "Hello, SpriteKit!";
simpleLabel.fontSize = 40;
simpleLabel.position = CGPoint(x: size.width / 2.0, y: size.height / 2.0)

addChild(simpleLabel)
```

As you look at this code, you can see that it first creates the SKLabelNode class by passing the init() method the name of the font you want to use. After that, you set the text property of the label. You then set the fontSize and position properties. Finally, you add the label node to the scene.

Let's give this a try in a sample application. Go back to Xcode and create a new Game project using Swift as the language. Now, just as you did in Chapter 1, delete the GameScene. sks and Actions.sks files. Open GameViewController.swift and replace its contents with the class in Listing 7-1.

© James Goodwill and Wesley Matlock 2017
J. Goodwill and W. Matlock, *Beginning Swift Games Development for iOS*,
DOI 10.1007/978-1-4842-2310-9_7

*Listing 7-1. GameViewController.swift: The Main UIViewController*

```swift
import SpriteKit

class GameViewController: UIViewController {

    var scene: GameScene!

    override func viewDidLoad() {

        super.viewDidLoad()

        // 1. Configure the main view
        let skView = view as! SKView
        skView.showsFPS = true

        // 2. Create and configure our game scene
        scene = GameScene(size: skView.bounds.size)
        scene.scaleMode = .aspectFill

        // 3. Show the scene.
        skView.presentScene(scene)
    }
}
```

When you have your GameViewController modified, go to the GameScene.swift file and change its body to match Listing 7-2.

*Listing 7-2. The New GameScene Class*

```swift
import SpriteKit

class GameScene: SKScene {

    required init?(coder aDecoder: NSCoder) {

        fatalError("init(coder:) has not been implemented")
    }

    override init(size: CGSize) {

        super.init(size: size)

        let simpleLabel = SKLabelNode(fontNamed: "Copperplate")
        simpleLabel.text = "Hello, SpriteKit!"
        simpleLabel.fontSize = 40
        simpleLabel.position = CGPoint(x: size.width / 2.0, y: size.height / 2.0)

        addChild(simpleLabel)
    }
}
```

Note this listing contains two init() methods. The first one is required and takes an NSCoder. Because we're managing the scene manually, you can ignore this init() method. The second init() method takes a CGSize. Inside the init() method this super.init() method is called, and then you see the SKLabel-related code.

This code looks exactly like the earlier snippet that added an SKLabelNode. Run the app and take a look at the results. The new app should look like Figure 7-1.

*Figure 7-1. A simple SKLabelNode example*

As you can see, the SKLabelNode is pretty easy to use. Most of SKLabelNode's properties are straightforward, but there are a couple of properties that you may not have seen. The two SKLabelNode properties are horizontalAlignmentMode and horizontalVerticalMode. Each of these properties is described in the following sections.

## Changing the Horizontal Alignment of the Label Node

SKLabelNode's horizontalAlignmentMode is used to set the horizontal position of the text relative to the node's position. There are three horizontal alignment options, all of which are defined by the enum SKLabelHorizontalAlignmentMode. The three options are SKLabelHorizontalAlignmentMode.left, SKLabelHorizontalAlignmentMode.center, and

SKLabelHorizontalAlignmentMode.right. To see how this property and these options change the layout of the label node, add the following line of code immediately after the line where you set the position of the label node:

```
simpleLabel.horizontalAlignmentMode = SKLabelHorizontalAlignmentMode.left
```

Now run the app again. This time you'll see that the label has been shifted to the right, as shown in Figure 7-2.

*Figure 7-2. A simple SKLabelNode example with its horizontalAlignmentMode set to SKLabelHorizontalAlignmentMode.right*

Setting this alignment to SKLabelHorizontalAlignmentMode.left tells SpriteKit to place the left side of the SKLabelNode at the origin of the label node.

The default value for the horizontalAlignmentMode is SKLabelHorizontalAlignmentMode. center, which places the center of the label at the position property of the label. You saw this mode in Figure 7-1.

Try one more thing before moving on. Change the value of the horizontalAlignmentMode property from SKLabelHorizontalAlignmentMode.left to SKLabelHorizontalAlignmentMode. right, as shown here, and run the app again:

```
simpleLabel.horizontalAlignmentMode = SKLabelHorizontalAlignmentMode.right
```

This time the right side of the label is place at the point of the SKLabelNode's position property, as shown in Figure 7-3.

*Figure 7-3. A simple SKLabelNode example with its horizontalAlignmentMode set to SKLabelHorizontalAlignmentMode.left*

# Changing the Vertical Alignment of the Label Node

In the previous section, you saw how you can change the horizontal alignment of the SKLabelNode using SKLabelNode's horizontalAlignmentMode property. In this section, you will see how you can change SKLabelNode's vertical alignment.

Before getting started, go back to the GameScene.swift file and change its contents so they match Listing 7-3.

*Listing 7-3. The GameScene Class with the Simple Label at the Top of the Scene*

```
import SpriteKit

class GameScene: SKScene {
```

```
required init?(coder aDecoder: NSCoder) {
    fatalError("init(coder:) has not been implemented")
}

override init(size: CGSize) {

    super.init(size: size)

    let simpleLabel = SKLabelNode(fontNamed: "Copperplate")
    simpleLabel.text = "Hello, SpriteKit!"
    simpleLabel.fontSize = 40
    simpleLabel.position =
        CGPoint(x: size.width / 2.0,
                y: frame.height - simpleLabel.frame.height)

    simpleLabel.horizontalAlignmentMode = SKLabelHorizontalAlignmentMode.center

    addChild(simpleLabel)
}
}
```

Note that this looks like the code you used in the previous section, except that the
SKLabelNode has been positioned at the top of the scene, and horizontalAlignmentMode has
been explicitly set to the center. To see how this looks, run the application again. It should
now look like Figure 7-4.

*Figure 7-4. The simple SKLabelNode at the top center of the scene*

The reason we moved the label to the top of the scene was so you can more easily see how changing the vertical alignment affects the node's presentation.

The SKLabelNode property you use to change the vertical alignment is verticalAlignmentMode. There are four values you can set this property to, and they're defined by the SKLabelVerticalAlignmentMode enum.

The first option, SKLabelVerticalAlignmentMode.baseline, is the default value and positions the text so that the font's baseline is on the node's origin. You already saw an example of this option in Figure 7-4 when verticalAlignmentMode was not set, which resulted in the use of the default value SKLabelVerticalAlignmentMode.baseline.

The second option is the SKLabelVerticalAlignmentMode enum value SKLabelVerticalAlignmentMode.center, which is used to center the text vertically on the node's origin. To see how the value changes the text layout, add the following line to the GameScene init() method right before you add the simpleLabel to the scene:

```
simpleLabel.verticalAlignmentMode = SKLabelVerticalAlignmentMode.center
```

Once you've made this change, run the application again. You'll now see that the text has shifted down so that the vertical center of the text is at the simpleLabel's origin, as shown in Figure 7-5.

*Figure 7-5. The simple SKLabelNode example with its verticalAlignmentMode set to SKLabelVerticalAlignmentMode.center*

The next vertical alignment option is the value SKLabelVerticalAlignmentMode.top. This value is used to position the text so that the top of the text is on the node's origin. To see how the value changes the text layout, set simpleLabel's verticalAlignmentMode value to SKLabelVerticalAlignmentMode.top, like this:

```
simpleLabel.verticalAlignmentMode = SKLabelVerticalAlignmentMode.top
```

Once you've made this change, run the application again. You'll now see that the text has shifted down even further so that the top of the text is at simpleLabel's origin, as shown in Figure 7-6.

*Figure 7-6. The simple SKLabelNode example with its verticalAlignmentMode set to SKLabelVerticalAlignmentMode.top*

The last vertical alignment option is the value SKLabelVerticalAlignmentMode.bottom. This value is used to position the text so that the bottom of the text is on the node's origin. To see how the value changes the text layout, set simpleLabel's verticalAlignmentMode to SKLabelVerticalAlignmentMode.bottom, as shown here:

```
simpleLabel.verticalAlignmentMode = SKLabelVerticalAlignmentMode.bottom
```

Once you've made this change, run the application again. You'll now see that the text has shifted up so that the bottom of the text is at simpleLabel's origin, as shown in Figure 7-7.

*Figure 7-7.* *The simple SKLabelNode example with its verticalAlignmentMode set to SKLabelVerticalAlignmentMode.bottom*

# Adding Scoring to the Game

Now that you know how to use SKLabelNode, it's time to put it to some good use. As mentioned at the beginning of this book, the goal of this game is to collect as many orbs as you can without colliding with a black hole or running out of impulses.

In this section, you'll finally add some scoring to the game. Specifically, you'll add an SKLabelNode to the top right of the scene. The original text will be "SCORE : 0." This numeric value will increment each time the playerNode comes into contact with an orb node—the more orbs collected, the higher your score. Let's make this happen by going back to the SuperSpaceman project.

The first step you need to take to add a scoring label to the GameScene is to create a variable to hold the score (the number of orbs collected) and an SKLabelNode constant to hold the label. You can accomplish that with the following two lines of code:

```
var score = 0
let scoreTextNode = SKLabelNode(fontNamed: "Copperplate")
```

This code is pretty straightforward. It creates an integer variable named score and sets it to 0, which makes sense at the beginning of a game, and then it creates an SKLabelNode with a font of Copperplate. We chose Copperplate because we thought it looked good with the images already in place, but you can choose whatever you like. After looking at this code, add it to the end of the GameScene's declaration section immediately before the first init() method:

```
var score = 0
let scoreTextNode = SKLabelNode(fontNamed: "Copperplate")

required init?(coder aDecoder: NSCoder) {

    super.init(coder: aDecoder)
}
```

The next thing you need to do is set all of the SKLabelNode's properties and add it to the GameScene. This is accomplished in the following snippet:

```
scoreTextNode.text = "SCORE : \(score)"
scoreTextNode.fontSize = 20
scoreTextNode.fontColor = SKColor.white
scoreTextNode.position =
                    CGPoint(x: size.width - 10, y: size.height - 20)
scoreTextNode.horizontalAlignmentMode = SKLabelHorizontalAlignmentMode.right

addChild(scoreTextNode)
```

You've seen all this before, but let's go over it before moving on. The first line sets the text of the label to "SCORE :" plus the current value in the variable score. The second and third lines set the font size and font color, respectively.

The fourth and fifth lines in the snippet are important. The fourth line sets the position (origin) of the scoreTextNode to 10 points to the left of the right side of the scene and 20 points from the top of the scene. The fifth line of this snippet sets the node's horizontal alignment to SKLabelHorizontalAlignmentMode.right, which will result in the label node's right side being set 10 points from the far-right side of the scene.

After that, the scoreTextNode is added to the scene. Once you've taken a look at this code, add it to the bottom of the init(size: CGSize() method and let's move on.

You need to complete one last step before you can run the app again and start working on your high score. Find the didBegin(_ contact: SKPhysicsContact) method in the GameScene extension and change the if statement handling contact with the orb nodes to the following:

```
if nodeB.name == "POWER_UP_ORB"  {

    impulseCount += 1

    score += 1
    scoreTextNode.text = "SCORE : \(score)"

    nodeB.removeFromParent()
}
```

Once you've saved your changes, take a look at the two lines added before the node is removed. The first of these two lines increments the score by one, and the second of these two lines changes the text of the scoreTextNode to reflect this increment. Make sure you've made all these changes and run the game again. You'll now see the score label in the top-right corner of the scene, as shown in Figure 7-8.

*Figure 7-8. The GameScene with a score label*

Start tapping the screen and try to collect some orbs. Note that every time your player comes into contact with an orb, the score is incremented. The game finally has scoring.

# Adding an Impulse Counter to the Game

Now that you have scoring in place, it's time to start telling the player how many impulses they have left before they run out and start falling to their demise. This will be much like adding the score label from the previous section. The biggest difference is that you're going to align the impulse label at the top left of the scene.

To get started with this, the first thing you need to do is add a constant to hold the impulse count label in the declarations section of the GameScene. This line is shown here:

```
let impulseTextNode = SKLabelNode(fontNamed: "Copperplate")
```

Add this line directly after the definition of the scoreTextNode constant. Next, modify the properties of the impulseTextNode. The code to do this is in the following snippet:

```
impulseTextNode.text = "IMPULSES : \(impulseCount)"
impulseTextNode.fontSize = 20
impulseTextNode.fontColor = SKColor.white
impulseTextNode.position = CGPoint(x: 10.0, y: size.height - 20)
impulseTextNode.horizontalAlignmentMode = SKLabelHorizontalAlignmentMode.left

addChild(impulseTextNode)
```

You've seen all this before. This code sets the text of the node to "IMPULSES :" plus the value currently stored in the instance variable impulseCount. It then sets the font size to 20 and the color to white. After that, it sets the position of the label node to 10 points from the left side of the scene and 20 points from the top of the scene. The final property change sets horizontalAlignementMode to SKLabelHorizontalAlignmentMode.left so that the left side of the text is anchored to the node's origin. After that, the impulseTextNode is added to the scene. Add this snippet to bottom of the GameScene's init(size: CGSize) method and save your work.

There are two more changes you need to make to update the displayed impulse count. The first is to modify the text in the impulseTextNode to reflect each time the player collects an orb, and the second is to modify the impulseTextNode each time the player uses an impulse.

Starting with incrementing the impulse count, you need to modify the didBegin(_ contact: SKPhysicsContact) method again. Specifically, you need to modify the if statement that handles contact with orb nodes. Take a look at the following snippet:

```
if nodeB.name == "POWER_UP_ORB"  {

    impulseCount += 1
    impulseTextNode.text = "IMPULSES : \(impulseCount)"

    score += 1
    scoreTextNode.text = "SCORE : \(score)"

    nodeB.removeFromParent()
}
```

Everything is the same from the previous section except the line following the increment of the impulse count. This line sets the text of the impulseTextNode to "IMPULSES :" plus the value of the impulseCount variable that was just incremented on the line before. Make these changes to the if statement and save your changes.

The last change you need to make to display the current impulse count is to modify the impulseTextNode each time an impulse is used by the player. To do this, you need to go back to the GameScene's touchesBegan() method and modify the if statement that applies the impulse to the playerNode to look like the following snippet:

```
if impulseCount > 0 {

    playerNode.physicsBody?.applyImpulse(CGVector (dx: 0.0, dy: 40.0))
```

```
impulseCount -= 1
impulseTextNode.text = "IMPULSES : \(impulseCount)"

engineExhaust!.isHidden = false

Timer.scheduledTimer(timeInterval: 0.5, target: self,
    selector:#selector(GameScene.hideEngineExhaust(_:)) , userInfo: nil, repeats: false)
}
```

There's only one change to the body of this if statement, and that's the line following the decrement of the impulseCount instance variable. On this line, the impulseTextNode's text property is being modified just like you did before, except this time the text node will be set to "IMPULSES :" plus the recently decremented impulseCount. When you're finished looking at this snippet, save your changes and run the game again. You'll now see the addition of the impulse count label in the top-left corner, as shown in Figure 7-9.

*Figure 7-9. The GameScene with an impulse count label*

Go ahead and tap the screen a few times. Note how the impulse count label node decreases each time you tap the screen and increases each time you come into contact with an orb node.

# Adding Simple Sounds to the Game

There's one more thing to cover before moving on to the next chapter. As we're sure you've noticed, there's no sound in this game—boring. In this section, you'll revisit SKActions so that you can add the functionality to play a sound each time an orb node is collected.

The SKAction method you'll use to create the action to play a sound is the playSoundFileNamed() method. Its signature is shown here:

```
class func playSoundFileNamed(soundFile: String,
                    waitForCompletion wait: Bool) -> SKAction
```

This method takes the name of an audio file in your application bundle and a Bool that indicates whether you want to wait until the sound is finished playing before moving on to the next line of code. The file you pass to this method can be any of these formats and more: MP3, M4A, CAF, WAV. An example usage of this method is shown in the following two lines:

```
let playSoundAction = SKAction.playSoundFileNamed("sound.wav",
                                waitForCompletion: false)
runAction(playSoundAction)
```

These two lines will create an SKAction that will play the file sound.wav and move on before the sound has finished playing. Let's add some sound to the SuperSpaceMan game.

Before going any further, find the zip file you downloaded in Chapter 1. This file contained all the images you need, plus it has a folder named sounds. In this directory you'll find a file named orb_pop.wav. Copy this file into the SuperSpaceMan folder of your project.

Once you've added the sound file to your project, the first step is to create the SKAction that will play the sound. The following code does that:

```
let orbPopAction = SKAction.playSoundFileNamed("orb_pop.wav",
                                waitForCompletion: false)
```

This code creates a constant named orbPopAction that holds an SKAction that will play the sound file orb_pop.wav whenever the action is run. Add this line to the declarations section of the GameScene immediately before the first init() method:

```
let orbPopAction = SKAction.playSoundFileNamed("orb_pop.wav",
        waitForCompletion: false)

required init?(coder aDecoder: NSCoder) {

    super.init(coder: aDecoder)
}
```

You now have an action that will play the orb_pop.wav file.

It's now time to add the code to play the sounds. To do that, you need to make one more modification to the didBegin(_ contact: SKPhysicsContact) method to add the code to run your new action. Take a look at the modified if statement that handles orb contact, shown here:

```
if nodeB.name == "POWER_UP_ORB" {

    run(orbPopAction)

    impulseCount += 1
    impulseTextNode.text = "IMPULSES : \(impulseCount)"

    score += 1
    scoreTextNode.text = "SCORE : \(score)"

    nodeB.removeFromParent()
}
```

Here you can see a new line, at the beginning of the if statement, that runs the orbPopAction whenever the contacted node's name is POWER_UP_ORB. Make this change to the if statement and run the game again. Now every time the playerNode comes into contact with an orb node, the orb_pop.wav sound is played.

# Summary

In this chapter, you saw how you can use SKLabelNodes to add labels to your SpriteKit games. Specifically, you saw how you can display the remaining number of impulses and how to add scoring to the game to keep up with the number of orbs the spaceman has collected. At the end of the chapter, you got a chance to revisit SKActions when you added sound to the game.

In the next chapter, you'll get a chance to add new scenes to the game and do some scene transitions when you add menuing and the ability to start a new game.

# Chapter 8

# Transitioning Between Scenes

In this chapter you'll learn how to implement scene transitions using SpriteKit's SKTransition class. You'll get a look at some of the different types of built-in transitions SpriteKit makes available to you. And you'll see how you can control each scene during a transition. At the end of the chapter, you'll take your newfound knowledge and add a menu scene to your SuperSpaceMan game.

As you already know, SKScenes are the components you use to present game content to users, and a well-designed game will group related content into individual scenes. For example, you could use different scenes to present different levels of a game, or you could use a scene to present a menu of options to a player.

To provide smooth transitions between scenes, SpriteKit provides the SKTransition class. Using SKTransitions is accomplished using three steps:

1. Create the SKScene you want to transition into.

2. Use one of the class-level SKTransition methods to create the transition you want to use.

3. Use the SKView's presentScene() method to present the new scene.

You can create your own custom transitions using the SKTransition's init() method, but it's more common to use one of the 13 built-in class-level SKTransition methods:

```
class func crossFade(withDuration: TimeInterval)
class func doorsCloseHorizontal(withDuration: TimeInterval)
class func doorsCloseVertical(withDuration: TimeInterval)
class func doorsOpenHorizontal(withDuration: TimeInterval)
class func doorsOpenVertical(withDuration: TimeInterval)
class func doorway(withDuration: TimeInterval)
class func fade(with: UIColor, duration: TimeInterval)
```

```
class func fade(withDuration: TimeInterval)
class func flipHorizontal(withDuration: TimeInterval)
class func flipVertical(withDuration: TimeInterval)
class func moveIn(with: SKTransitionDirection, duration: TimeInterval)
class func push(with: SKTransitionDirection, duration: TimeInterval)
class func reveal(with: SKTransitionDirection, duration: TimeInterval)
```

As you can see, SpriteKit provides a pretty complete set of built-in transitions. An example use of one of these transitions is shown in the following snippet:

```
let transition = SKTransition.fade(withDuration: 2.0)
let sceneTwo = SceneTwo(size: size)

view?.presentScene(sceneTwo, transition: transition)
```

Take a look at this code. The first line of this snippet creates a transition that will fade to black and then fade to a new scene over a two-second duration. The second line creates the scene you will be transitioning into, and the final line actually presents the scene using the transition.

# Pausing Scenes During a Transition

You should be aware of two important SKTransition properties when transitioning between scenes: pausesIncomingScene and pausesOutgoingScene. These properties are Bool properties used to pause the animation of the incoming and outgoing scenes, respectively.

If you want a scene's animations to continue during scene transitions, you just set the appropriate property to false before you present the scene. The default value for both properties is true.

# Detecting When a New Scene Is Presented

SpriteKit provides two methods in the SKScene class that you can override to detect when a scene is being transitioned away from or transitioned into. The first method is the SKScene willMove () method. This method is called on an SKScene when it is about to be removed from a view. To override this method, you add the following code to your SKScene implementation:

```
override func willMove(from: SKView) {

    // insert code
}
```

The second method is the SKScene didMove () method. This method is called when the scene has just finished being presented by a view. To override this method, you add the following code to your SKScene implementation:

```
override func didMove(to: SKView) {

    // insert code
}
```

# Adding a New Scene to SuperSpaceMan

In this section, you will use your newfound knowledge of scene transitions and add a new scene to the SuperSpaceMan game. The purpose of this scene will be to allow the user to see the score of their most recent game and let them start a new game.

Before you do anything, let's add a simple message that tells the game player to tap the screen to start the game. As you know, the game already starts when you tap the screen. This label is just nice to have to start tidying up the user interface. To add this label, go to the GameScene's declaration section and add the following line of code directly before the first init() method:

```
let startGameTextNode = SKLabelNode(fontNamed: "Copperplate")
```

After you've added this line, go to the bottom of the GameScene's init(size: CGSize) method and add the following block of code to the bottom of this method:

```
startGameTextNode.text = "TAP ANYWHERE TO START!"
startGameTextNode.horizontalAlignmentMode = SKLabelHorizontalAlignmentMode.center
startGameTextNode.verticalAlignmentMode = SKLabelVerticalAlignmentMode.center
startGameTextNode.fontSize = 20
startGameTextNode.fontColor = SKColor.white
startGameTextNode.position =
    CGPoint(x: scene!.size.width / 2, y: scene!.size.height / 2)
addChild(startGameTextNode)
```

Note that you saw code similar to this in Chapter 7. Once you look at the changes, run the game again. You'll now see a new label of "TAP ANYWHERE TO START!" in white letters at the center of the scene, as shown in Figure 8-1.

*Figure 8-1.*   *The GameScene with the "TAP ANYWHERE TO START!" SKLabelNode*

Before moving on, do one more thing: add the code to remove the `startGameTextNode` label from the scene when the screen is tapped. You can do this by adding the following line to the first `if` statement in the `touchedBegan()` method:

```
startGameTextNode.removeFromParent()
```

# Ending the Game

Now it's time to add the code that will determine when the SuperSpaceMan game ends. There are really only two ways the game ends; either the player dodges all the black holes and collects orbs until he reaches the top of the scene and wins or he falls off the bottom of the scene and loses. The easiest place to check the player's position as it updates is in the `GameScene`'s `update()` method. Let's go back to that method and add the necessary code to do this.

Currently, the `update()` method has a simple `if` statement that moves the foreground and background nodes according to the `playerNode`'s position as long as the `playerNode`'s y-position is greater than or equal to 180.0. This means the `playerNode` could leave the `backgroundNodes` behind and fly off into the black of space. We really don't like the way that looks. To stop this from happening, modify the current `if` statement to look like the following:

```
if playerNode.position.y >= 180.0 &&
    playerNode.position.y < 6400.0 {
```

Save this change and run the game again. Try making it to the top of the game and see what happens. This time, when you reach the top of the scene, the background and foreground will stop moving, and the `playerNode` will continue out of the viewport. This is a little better.

# Winning the Game

At this point, you know that the player is about to fly off the top of the scene, but you need to test to see when the player actually flies off the scene to determine whether he actually wins. To do this, add the following `else if` to the current `if` block in the `update()` method:

```
else if playerNode.position.y > 7000.0 {

    gameOverWithResult(true)
}
```

This code checks to see whether the `playerNode` has flown more than 7,000 points up the scene. If it has, it calls a new instance method `gameOverWithResult()`, passing `true` to this method, which indicates that the player won. Make these changes, and let's take a look at the `gameOverWithResult()` method shown here:

```
func gameOverWithResult(_ gameResult: Bool) {

    playerNode.removeFromParent()

    if gameResult {

        print("YOU WON!")
    }
    else {

        print("YOU LOSE!")
    }
}
```

Note that it doesn't do a whole lot at the moment. It first removes the `playerNode` from the scene and then it sets node to `nil`. After that, it tests the `gameResult` `Bool` passed to it and prints whether the player won the game.

Don't worry too much about this method at the moment. You'll be modifying this code soon enough. For now, add this method to the bottom of the `GameScene`, and let's get to determining whether the player lost the game.

> **Note**   Numbers like 6400.0 and 7000.0 may seem like crazy numbers when the height of
> the display is nowhere near either of these. Remember, you added the playerNode to the
> foregroundNode, and you've been moving the foregroundNode down while the playerNode,
> virtually, continues up the scene. This is how the player's y-position is so much higher than the
> height of the device's viewport.

# Losing the Game

You now know when the player has won the game. It's now time to test to see whether the
player has lost the game. To do that, go back to the update() method and add the following
else if to the bottom of the if statement (directly following the else if you just added):

```
else if playerNode.position.y < 0.0 {

    gameOverWithResult(false)
}
```

This bit of code is pretty easy to understand. If the playerNode's y-position is less than
0.0, then the player has fallen off the bottom of the scene, and the gameOverWithResult()
method is called with the value false being passed to it, which indicates that the player has
lost the game.

There's one last thing you need to do before transitioning to a new scene. In the
gameOverWithResult() method, you removed the playerNode from the parent and set it
to nil. That's perfectly fine, but you need to make sure you don't try to use this property
without first checking to see whether it's nil. There are only two places you currently do this.

The first is in the update() method with each time you're checking the playerNode's position.
To make sure you don't dereference a nil playerNode, you need to surround the body of the
update() method with an if, checking to make sure the playerNode property isn't nil. You
can see this change in the new update() method shown here:

```
override func update(_ currentTime: TimeInterval) {

    if playerNode.position.y >= 180.0 {

        backgroundNode.position =
            CGPoint(x: backgroundNode.position.x,
                    y: -((playerNode.position.y - 180.0)/8));

        backgroundStarsNode.position =
            CGPoint(x: backgroundStarsNode.position.x,
                    y: -((playerNode.position.y - 180.0)/6));

        backgroundPlanetNode.position =
            CGPoint(x: backgroundPlanetNode.position.x,
                    y: -((playerNode.position.y - 180.0)/8));
```

```
        foregroundNode.position =
            CGPoint(x: foregroundNode.position.x,
                    y: -(playerNode.position.y - 180.0));
    }
    else if playerNode.position.y > 7000.0 {

        gameOverWithResult(true)
    }
    else if playerNode.position.y + playerNode.size.height < 0.0 {

        gameOverWithResult(false)
    }
}
```

After taking a look at these changes, modify your update() to look like this one, and let's move on to adding the actual transition.

# Adding the Transition

Before you can transition to a new scene, you need to have a scene to transition to. The scene this game needs is a scene that tells the player the score they achieved in the most recent game and lets them play a new game.

To create the new scene, select the File ➤ New ➤ File menu item and then choose iOS ➤ Source ➤ Swift File; click the Next button. Make sure you have the SuperSpaceMan folder selected, name the file MenuScene, and click Create. You'll now have an almost empty new file named MenuScene.swift. Replace its contents with the contents of Listing 8-1.

*Listing 8-1. MenuScene.swift: The SuperSpaceMan MenuScene*

```
import SpriteKit

class MenuScene: SKScene {

    required init?(coder aDecoder: NSCoder) {

        super.init(coder: aDecoder)
    }

    init(size: CGSize, gameResult: Bool, score: Int) {

        super.init(size: size)

        let backgroundNode = SKSpriteNode(imageNamed: "Background")
        backgroundNode.size.width = self.frame.size.width
        backgroundNode.position = CGPoint(x: size.width / 2, y: 0.0)
        backgroundNode.anchorPoint = CGPoint(x: 0.5, y: 0.0)
        addChild(backgroundNode)

        let gameResultTextNode = SKLabelNode(fontNamed: "Copperplate")
        gameResultTextNode.text = "YOU " + (gameResult ? "WON" : "LOST")
        gameResultTextNode.horizontalAlignmentMode =
            SKLabelHorizontalAlignmentMode.center
```

```
    gameResultTextNode.verticalAlignmentMode =
        SKLabelVerticalAlignmentMode.center
    gameResultTextNode.fontSize = 20
    gameResultTextNode.fontColor = SKColor.white
    gameResultTextNode.position =
        CGPoint(x: size.width / 2.0, y: size.height - 200.0)
    addChild(gameResultTextNode)

    let scoreTextNode = SKLabelNode(fontNamed: "Copperplate")
    scoreTextNode.text = "SCORE :  \(score)"
    scoreTextNode.horizontalAlignmentMode =
        SKLabelHorizontalAlignmentMode.center
    scoreTextNode.verticalAlignmentMode =
        SKLabelVerticalAlignmentMode.center
    scoreTextNode.fontSize = 20
    scoreTextNode.fontColor = SKColor.white
    scoreTextNode.position = CGPoint(x: size.width / 2.0,
        y: gameResultTextNode.position.y - 40.0)
    addChild(scoreTextNode)

    let tryAgainTextNodeLine1 = SKLabelNode(fontNamed: "Copperplate")
    tryAgainTextNodeLine1.text = "TAP ANYWHERE"
    tryAgainTextNodeLine1.horizontalAlignmentMode =
        SKLabelHorizontalAlignmentMode.center
    tryAgainTextNodeLine1.verticalAlignmentMode =
        SKLabelVerticalAlignmentMode.center
    tryAgainTextNodeLine1.fontSize = 20
    tryAgainTextNodeLine1.fontColor = SKColor.white
    tryAgainTextNodeLine1.position = CGPoint(x: size.width / 2.0, y: 100.0)
    addChild(tryAgainTextNodeLine1)

    let tryAgainTextNodeLine2 = SKLabelNode(fontNamed: "Copperplate")
    tryAgainTextNodeLine2.text = "TO PLAY AGAIN!"
    tryAgainTextNodeLine2.horizontalAlignmentMode =
        SKLabelHorizontalAlignmentMode.center
    tryAgainTextNodeLine2.verticalAlignmentMode =
        SKLabelVerticalAlignmentMode.center
    tryAgainTextNodeLine2.fontSize = 20
    tryAgainTextNodeLine2.fontColor = SKColor.white
    tryAgainTextNodeLine2.position = CGPoint(x: size.width / 2.0,
        y: tryAgainTextNodeLine1.position.y - 40.0)
    addChild(tryAgainTextNodeLine2)
}

override func touchesBegan(_ touches: Set<UITouch>, with event: UIEvent?) {

    let transition = SKTransition.doorsOpenHorizontal(withDuration: 2.0)
    let gameScene = GameScene(size: size)

    view?.presentScene(gameScene, transition: transition)
}
}
```

Note that the second init() method takes three parameters: the size of the scene, the result of the game as a Bool, and the player's score. The size parameter, as you know, is used to set the size of the scene, and the third and fourth parameters will be used to display information about the result of the game to the user.

Inside the init() method, it starts off by adding a background image. The image used is the same image you used in the GameScene. After that, it adds several labels to the scene, including two labels that are added to the middle of the scene. The first tells the user whether they won or lost the game, and the second tells them their score. Next, two labels are added to the bottom of the scene, telling the player to tap the screen anywhere to play again. Once you've added the code to the MenuScene.swift file, save your work, and let's go back to the GameScene.swift file.

You now have a scene to transition to, so let's add the code to perform the transition. The code to make this transition is shown in the following snippet:

```
let transition = SKTransition.crossFade(withDuration: 2.0)
let menuScene = MenuScene(size: size,
                          gameResult: gameResult,
                          score: score)

view?.presentScene(menuScene, transition: transition)
```

The first line of this snippet creates a cross-fade transition that will fade in the scene over a two-second duration. The second line creates the MenuScene itself, passing it the size of the current scene followed by the result of the game and the player's score. The third line of this snippet actually presents the MenuScene, which replaces the current scene using the transition created on the first line. After reading this code, add it to the bottom of the GameScene's gameOverWithResult() method, as shown here:

```
func gameOverWithResult(_ gameResult: Bool) {

    playerNode.removeFromParent()

    let transition = SKTransition.crossFade(withDuration: 2.0)
    let menuScene = MenuScene(size: size,
                    gameResult: gameResult,
                        score: score)

    view?.presentScene(menuScene, transition: transition)
}
```

Now run the game and either play to win or play to lose. Either way, you'll see the new scene fade in, as shown in Figure 8-2, when the game is over.

*Figure 8-2. The MenuScene when the game is over*

Awesome. You've now added a simple scene transition that communicates whether the player won or lost the game and what their score was when the game ended.

There's one last change you need to make before moving on to the next chapter: add another transition that will start a new game when the player taps the MenuScene. The code to do this is shown in the following override of the MenuScene's touchesBegan() method:

```
override func touchesBegan(_ touches: Set<UITouch>, with event: UIEvent?) {

    let transition = SKTransition.doorsOpenHorizontal(withDuration: 2.0)
    let gameScene = GameScene(size: size)

    view?.presentScene(gameScene, transition: transition)
}
```

This method creates a doorsOpenHorizontalWithDuration transition and a new instance of the GameScene and then presents the new GameScene using the new transition. Add this method to the bottom of the MenuScene class and run the application again. This time, when the game is over and you are presented with the MenuScene, tap the screen, and you'll be able to play another game.

# Summary

In this chapter, you learned how to implement scene transitions using SpriteKit's SKTransition class. You looked at some of the different types of built-in transitions SpriteKit makes available to you. You also saw how you could control each scene during a transition. At the end of the chapter, you took your new knowledge of scene transitions and added a menu scene to your SuperSpaceMan game.

In Chapter 9 you'll be wrapping up your study of SpriteKit programming with Swift when you focus on SpriteKit best practices. At the end of the chapter, you'll spend just a little time cleaning up the SuperSpaceMan application when you do some refactoring.

# SpriteKit Best Practices

In this chapter, you'll learn some SpriteKit best practices; specifically, you'll see how you can create your own subclasses of SKSpriteNode so that you can better reuse your nodes. You'll then move on to changing your game to load all the sprites into a single texture atlas that you can reference when creating all future sprites. After that, you'll move on to externalizing some of your game data so that designers and testers can change the game play. Finally, you'll close out the chapter when you prune your node tree of all nodes that have fallen off the bottom of the screen.

## Creating Your Own Nodes with Subclassing

The first best practice we want to talk about is refactoring your sprite nodes into their own classes. Doing this will both clean up your scene code and encapsulate each node's specific code to its own class.

The three nodes that can be abstracted to their own classes are the player, orb, and black hole nodes. Before you can start this process, you need to create a new file to share constants. The purpose of this file is to hold all the collision categories that will be used across each of the nodes.

Create this new file and name it SharedConstants.swift. Once this file is in place, move all the collision categories from the GameScene.swift file to this file. When you're finished, your new file should look like Listing 9-1.

*Listing 9-1. SharedConstants.swift: A File to Hold Constant Used in Multiple Classes*

```
let CollisionCategoryPlayer : UInt32 = 0x1 << 1
let CollisionCategoryPowerUpOrbs : UInt32 = 0x1 << 2
let CollisionCategoryBlackHoles : UInt32 = 0x1 << 3
```

After you have the constants set up, create another new file, named SpaceMan.swift. This is the file that will hold your refactored playerNode's class. Once you've created the file, copy the code in Listing 9-2 into it and save your work.

© James Goodwill and Wesley Matlock 2017
J. Goodwill and W. Matlock, *Beginning Swift Games Development for iOS*,
DOI 10.1007/978-1-4842-2310-9_9

*Listing 9-2. SpaceMan.swift: The New SpaceMan Class*

```swift
import Foundation
import SpriteKit

class SpaceMan: SKSpriteNode {

    required init?(coder aDecoder: NSCoder) {
        fatalError("init(coder:) has not been implemented")
    }

    init() {

        let texture = SKTexture(imageNamed: "Player")
        super.init(texture: texture, color: UIColor.clear, size: texture.size())

        physicsBody = SKPhysicsBody(circleOfRadius: size.width / 2)
        physicsBody?.isDynamic = false
        physicsBody?.linearDamping = 1.0
        physicsBody?.allowsRotation = false

        physicsBody?.categoryBitMask = CollisionCategoryPlayer
        physicsBody?.contactTestBitMask = CollisionCategoryPowerUpOrbs |
        CollisionCategoryBlackHoles
        physicsBody?.collisionBitMask = 0
    }
}
```

The SpaceMan class extends SKSpriteNode, and all the code related to setting up the spaceman's texture and physicsBody has been moved into the spaceman's init() method. The one thing to note is that, at the beginning of the init() method, we create a texture with the Player image and then you call the required super.init() method. That's because we're subclassing SKSpriteNode, and this is the required init(). We talk a lot more about textures in a later section in this chapter.

Now that we have everything moved to this class, it will be much easier to use in a game scene. Once you have the new SpaceMan class, you can remove the following snippet of nine lines of code in the GameScene:

```swift
playerNode.physicsBody = SKPhysicsBody(circleOfRadius: playerNode.size.width / 2)
playerNode.physicsBody?.dynamic = false

playerNode.position = CGPoint(x: size.width / 2.0, y: 220.0)
playerNode.physicsBody?.linearDamping = 1.0
playerNode.physicsBody?.allowsRotation = false

playerNode.physicsBody?.categoryBitMask = CollisionCategoryPlayer

playerNode.physicsBody?.contactTestBitMask = CollisionCategoryPowerUpOrbs |
CollisionCategoryBlackHoles
playerNode.physicsBody?.collisionBitMask = 0
```

After removing the previous snippet from GameScene's init(size: CGSize) method, be sure to leave the following line in place:

```
playerNode.position = CGPoint(x: size.width / 2.0, y: 220.0)
```

The last thing you need to do to use your new SpaceMan class is change the declaration of the node from:

```
let playerNode = SKSpriteNode(imageNamed: "Player")
```

to:

```
let playerNode = SpaceMan()
```

The next class you need to create is a class that will encapsulate all the orb node–related code. To do that, create another file, named Orb.swift, and copy the contents of Listing 9-3 into it.

*Listing 9-3. Orb.swift: The New Orb Class*

```
import Foundation
import SpriteKit

class Orb: SKSpriteNode {

    required init?(coder aDecoder: NSCoder) {
        fatalError("init(coder:) has not been implemented")
    }

    init() {

        let texture = SKTexture(imageNamed: "PowerUp")
        super.init(texture: texture,
                   color: UIColor.clear,
                   size: texture.size())

        physicsBody =
            SKPhysicsBody(circleOfRadius: self.size.width / 2)
        physicsBody?.isDynamic = false

        physicsBody?.categoryBitMask = CollisionCategoryPowerUpOrbs
        physicsBody?.collisionBitMask = 0
        name = "POWER_UP_ORB"
    }
}
```

This new Orb class, much like the SpaceMan class, contains all the code to set up the node's texture and its physicsBody. Once you have the new Orb class in place, you can then change the addOrbsToForeground() method to look like the following simplified method:

```
func addOrbsToForeground() {

    var orbNodePosition =
        CGPoint(x: playerNode.position.x, y: playerNode.position.y + 100)
    var orbXShift : CGFloat = -1.0

    for _ in 0...49 {

        // new code to use an orb
        let orbNode = Orb()

        if orbNodePosition.x - (orbNode.size.width * 2) <= 0 {

            orbXShift = 1.0
        }

        if orbNodePosition.x + orbNode.size.width >= size.width {

            orbXShift = -1.0
        }

        orbNodePosition.x += 40.0 * orbXShift
        orbNodePosition.y += 120
        orbNode.position = orbNodePosition

        foregroundNode.addChild(orbNode)
    }
}
```

The addOrbsToForeground() method is now much simpler. It performs only three steps: it creates each of the orb nodes, sets their respective positions, and then adds them to the scene.

The last node class you're going to create is the BlackHole class. As you can probably guess, this class will contain all the code related to a black hole. Create another new file named BlackHole.swift and copy the contents of Listing 9-4 into it.

*Listing 9-4. BlackHole.swift: The New BlackHole Class*

```
import Foundation
import SpriteKit

class BlackHole: SKSpriteNode {

    required init?(coder aDecoder: NSCoder) {
        fatalError("init(coder:) has not been implemented")
    }
```

```
init() {

    let frame0 = SKTexture(imageNamed: "BlackHole0")
    let frame1 = SKTexture(imageNamed: "BlackHole1")
    let frame2 = SKTexture(imageNamed: "BlackHole2")
    let frame3 = SKTexture(imageNamed: "BlackHole3")
    let frame4 = SKTexture(imageNamed: "BlackHole4")

    let blackHoleTextures = [frame0, frame1, frame2, frame3, frame4]
    let animateAction =
        SKAction.animate(with: blackHoleTextures, timePerFrame: 0.2)

    let rotateAction = SKAction.repeatForever(animateAction)

    super.init(texture: frame0,
               color: UIColor.clear,
               size: frame0.size())

    physicsBody = SKPhysicsBody(circleOfRadius: size.width / 2)
    physicsBody?.isDynamic = false
    physicsBody?.categoryBitMask = CollisionCategoryBlackHoles
    physicsBody?.collisionBitMask = 0
    name = "BLACK_HOLE"

    run(rotateAction)
    }
}
```

Once you have the new BlackHole class in place, you can then change the
addBlackHolesToForeground() method to look like the following simplified method:

```
func addBlackHolesToForeground() {

    let moveLeftAction = SKAction.moveTo(x: 0.0, duration: 2.0)
    let moveRightAction = SKAction.moveTo(x: size.width, duration: 2.0)
    let actionSequence = SKAction.sequence([moveLeftAction, moveRightAction])
    let moveAction = SKAction.repeatForever(actionSequence)

    for i in 1...10 {

        // new black hole usage code
        let blackHoleNode = BlackHole()

        blackHoleNode.position = CGPoint(x: size.width - 80.0, y: 600.0 * CGFloat(i))
        blackHoleNode.run(moveAction)

        foregroundNode.addChild(blackHoleNode)
    }
}
```

Moving these nodes into their own classes makes it a lot easier to reuse each of the nodes
and also cleans up the GameScene.

# Reusing Textures

The next best practice you're going to see is how you can use a single instance of an SKTextureAtlas to load all the sprite images and then just reuse the atlas when setting all your sprite's textures. The first step to make this happen is to create an SKTextureAtlas and pass it to nodes so they can retrieve their own textures. Add this line of code immediately before the first init() method in the GameScene class:

```
let textureAtlas = SKTextureAtlas(named: "sprites.atlas")
```

After you've created the texture atlas, you need to change the init() method of each of the recently created SKSpriteNodes to take an SKTextureAtlas as a parameter. Once the SKSpriteNode has a reference to the SKTextureAtlas, then you can change the texture-loading code in each node to use this passed-in textureAtlas. The following init() method shows this change made to the SpaceMan class:

```
init(textureAtlas: SKTextureAtlas) {

    let texture = textureAtlas.textureNamed("Player")
    super.init(texture: texture, color: UIColor.clear, size: texture.size())

    physicsBody = SKPhysicsBody(circleOfRadius: size.width / 2)
    physicsBody?.isDynamic = false
    physicsBody?.linearDamping = 1.0
    physicsBody?.allowsRotation = false

    physicsBody?.categoryBitMask = CollisionCategoryPlayer
    physicsBody?.contactTestBitMask =
        CollisionCategoryPowerUpOrbs | CollisionCategoryBlackHoles
    physicsBody?.collisionBitMask = 0
}
```

Notice the init() method's parameter list now takes an SKTextureAtlas parameter, and the first line of the init() method uses this SKTextureAtlas to load the Player texture. Also note that the init() method no longer overrides the default init(), and therefore we've removed the override keyword. Make this change to the SpaceMan.swift's init() method and let's go back to GameScene class and change the playerNode declaration. To use the new SpaceMan.init() method, you will need to make a few changes.

In the GameScene class you'll first change the construction of the playerNode at the top of the class to look like the following line:

```
var playerNode: SpaceMan!
```

Next, add a line in the init() that will initialize the playerNode with the correct SpaceMan SKSpriteNode. Right above the code where you set the playerNode.position, add the following line:

```
playerNode = SpaceMan(textureAtlas: textureAtlas)
```

After you've made all the SpaceMan changes, let's move on to doing the same to both the Orb and BlackHole classes. First change the init() method of the Orb to take an SKTextureAtlas:

```
init(textureAtlas: SKTextureAtlas) {

    let texture = textureAtlas.textureNamed("PowerUp")
    super.init(texture: texture, color: UIColor.clear, size: texture.size())

    physicsBody = SKPhysicsBody(circleOfRadius: size.width / 2)
    physicsBody?.isDynamic = false

    physicsBody?.categoryBitMask = CollisionCategoryPowerUpOrbs
    physicsBody?.collisionBitMask = 0
    name = "POWER_UP_ORB"
}
```

After changing the Orb's init() method, change GameScene's addOrbsToForeground() to look like the following:

```
func addOrbsToForeground() {

    var orbNodePosition =
        CGPoint(x: playerNode.position.x, y: playerNode.position.y + 100)
    var orbXShift : CGFloat = -1.0

    for _ in 0...49 {

        let orbNode = Orb(textureAtlas: SKTextureAtlas(named: "sprites.atlas"))

        if orbNodePosition.x - (orbNode.size.width * 2) <= 0 {

            orbXShift = 1.0
        }

        if orbNodePosition.x + orbNode.size.width >= size.width {

            orbXShift = -1.0
        }

        orbNodePosition.x += 40.0 * orbXShift
        orbNodePosition.y += 120
        orbNode.position = orbNodePosition

        foregroundNode.addChild(orbNode)
    }
}
```

Next, change the `init()` method of the `BlackHole` to take an `SKTextureAtlas` and then use this texture atlas to load all the textures going forward. This change is shown in the following snippet:

```
init(textureAtlas: SKTextureAtlas) {

    let frame0 = textureAtlas.textureNamed("BlackHole0")
    let frame1 = textureAtlas.textureNamed("BlackHole1")
    let frame2 = textureAtlas.textureNamed("BlackHole2")
    let frame3 = textureAtlas.textureNamed("BlackHole3")
    let frame4 = textureAtlas.textureNamed("BlackHole4")

    let blackHoleTextures = [frame0, frame1, frame2, frame3, frame4];
    let animateAction = SKAction.animate(with: blackHoleTextures, timePerFrame: 0.2)

    let rotateAction = SKAction.repeatForever(animateAction)

    super.init(texture: frame0, color: UIColor.clear, size: frame0.size())

    physicsBody = SKPhysicsBody(circleOfRadius: size.width / 2)
    physicsBody?.isDynamic = false
    physicsBody?.categoryBitMask = CollisionCategoryBlackHoles
    physicsBody?.collisionBitMask = 0
    name = "BLACK_HOLE"

    run(rotateAction)
}
```

Finally, change `GameScene`'s `addBlackHolesToForeground()` so that it passes the `SKTextureAtlas` to the `BlackHole`, as shown here:

```
func addBlackHolesToForeground() {

    let moveLeftAction = SKAction.moveTo(x: 0.0, duration: 2.0)
    let moveRightAction = SKAction.moveTo(x: size.width, duration: 2.0)
    let actionSequence = SKAction.sequence([moveLeftAction, moveRightAction])
    let moveAction = SKAction.repeatForever(actionSequence)

    for i in 1...10 {

        // new black hole usage code
        let blackHoleNode = BlackHole(textureAtlas:
            SKTextureAtlas(named: "sprites.atlas"))

        blackHoleNode.position = CGPoint(x: size.width - 80.0,
                                         y: 600.0 * CGFloat(i))
        blackHoleNode.run(moveAction)

        foregroundNode.addChild(blackHoleNode)
    }
}
```

At this point, all the SKSpriteNodes reuse the same SKTextureAtlas, which will speed up the retrieval of each of your node's textures.

# Externalizing Your Game Data

The next best practice we want to talk about won't necessarily improve the performance of your game, but it will help during development and testing. So far, all the positions of each game node are hard-coded in the SuperSpaceMan Swift code. This is if you're creating a simple game, with you being both the designer and the developer of the game; if you have a team with clearly defined roles, you may want to make it possible for a designer or tester to change the play of the game without changing the Swift code. One way to do this is to externalize the positions of your game nodes.

A simple way to do this in the SuperSpaceMan game is to move the orb and black hole positions to plist files. You can then load the node positions using an NSBundle. This will make it possible for a designer or tester to just change a plist to change the layout of the whole game. An example plist that holds the first three orb node positions is shown here:

```
<?xml version="1.0" encoding="UTF-8"?>
<!DOCTYPE plist PUBLIC "-//Apple//DTD PLIST 1.0//EN" "http://www.apple.com/DTDs/
PropertyList-1.0.dtd">
<plist version="1.0">
<dict>
    <key>positions</key>
    <array>
    <dict>
        <key>x</key>
        <real>120.0</real>
        <key>y</key>
        <real>440.0</real>
    </dict>
    <dict>
        <key>x</key>
        <real>80.0</real>
        <key>y</key>
        <real>560.0</real>
    </dict>
    <dict>
        <key>x</key>
        <real>120.0</real>
        <key>y</key>
        <real>680.0</real>
    </dict>
    ...
    </array>
</dict>
</plist>
```

In this file, you can see an array of dictionaries each containing the x- and y-positions of the orb nodes. Don't worry about creating this file yourself. You can find an orbs.plist file and a blackholes.plist file in the previously downloaded zip file containing the images you used for your sprites. Copy both of these files into the SupportingFiles groups of your project, and let's move on to using each of these files.

Once you've copied both plist files into your project, you can then load them using the main bundle. Take a look at the following modified addOrbsToForeground() method:

```
func addOrbsToForeground() {

    let orbPlistPath = Bundle.main.path(forResource: "orbs", ofType: "plist")
    let orbDataDictionary = NSDictionary(contentsOfFile: orbPlistPath!)

    if let positionDictionary = orbDataDictionary {

        let positions = positionDictionary.object(forKey: "positions") as! NSArray

        for position in positions {

            let orbNode = Orb(textureAtlas: SKTextureAtlas(named: "sprites.atlas"))
            let x = (position as AnyObject).object(forKey: "x") as! CGFloat
            let y = (position as AnyObject).object(forKey: "y") as! CGFloat
            orbNode.position = CGPoint(x: x, y: y)
            foregroundNode.addChild(orbNode)
        }
    }
}
```

In the new addOrbsToForeground() method, you can see that it first loads the contents of orbs.plist. After that, it grabs the array of positions out of the dictionary, and finally it iterates over all the positions, adding each orbNode to the foregroundNode at that position. Now you can change the number and layout of all the orb nodes by simply changing the plist.

Make these changes to the addOrbsToForeground() method, and let's do the same thing with the black holes. You've already copied the blackholes.plist file into your project, so you can skip that step and move on to modifying the addBlackHolesToForeground() method to load the black hole positions from the plist. The new addBlackHolesToForeground() method is shown here:

```
func addBlackHolesToForeground() {

    let moveLeftAction = SKAction.moveTo(x: 0.0, duration: 2.0)
    let moveRightAction = SKAction.moveTo(x: size.width, duration: 2.0)
    let actionSequence = SKAction.sequence([moveLeftAction, moveRightAction])
    let moveAction = SKAction.repeatForever(actionSequence)

    let blackHolePlistPath = Bundle.main.path(forResource: "blackholes", ofType: "plist")
    let blackHoleDataDictionary = NSDictionary(contentsOfFile: blackHolePlistPath!)

    if let positionDictionary = blackHoleDataDictionary {
```

```
        let positions = positionDictionary.object(forKey: "positions") as! NSArray

        for position in positions {

            let blackHoleNode = BlackHole(textureAtlas: SKTextureAtlas(named: "sprites.atlas"))

            let x = (position as AnyObject).object(forKey: "x") as! CGFloat
            let y = (position as AnyObject).object(forKey: "y")as! CGFloat
            blackHoleNode.position = CGPoint(x: x, y: y)

            blackHoleNode.run(moveAction)

            foregroundNode.addChild(blackHoleNode)
        }
    }
}
}
```

Note that now the addBlackHolesToForeground() method, just like the addOrbsToForeground() method, reads all the black hole node positions from the plist and then adds each of the blackHoleNodes at those read-in positions. Make this change and run your game again. You'll see no difference, but now people with little to no development experience can completely change the game.

# Keeping Your Node Tree Pruned

The final best practice to implement in the SuperSpaceMan game is to remove all SKNodes that have dropped off the bottom of the viewable scene. Removing unnecessary nodes from your games will improve the overall performance of node tree rendering and reduce the amount of memory used to hold all the nodes in your node tree.

A simple way to remove unnecessary nodes from GameScene is to create a method that will remove all nodes with a given name that are one scene length below the playerNode. Take a look at the following removeOutOfSceneNodesWithName() method:

```
func removeOutOfSceneNodesWithName(_ name: String) {

    foregroundNode.enumerateChildNodes(withName: name, using: {
        node, stop in

        if self.playerNode.position.y - node.position.y > self.size.height {

            node.removeFromParent()
        }
    })
}
```

This method takes a single String representing the name of each SKNode you want to test and uses the enumerateChildNodesWithName() method to check to see whether those nodes are positioned one scene length below the playerNode. If the returned node is greater than one scene length, it's removed from the scene. Notice one thing about this method: inside the enumerateChildNodesWithName() method it first checks to see whether the playerNode is nil. If the playerNode is nil, then it stops the search for child nodes by setting the stop.memory property to true. Add this method to the bottom of the GameScene.

To use the removeOutOfSceneNodesWithName(), you need to add a call to this method, for each node that can be removed from the scene, to the bottom of GameScene's update() method. In this instance, the two nodes that can fall out of the scene are the BLACK_HOLE and POWER_UP_ORB nodes. Take a look at the modified update() method with these two calls added to the end of the method, shown here:

```
override func update(_ currentTime: TimeInterval) {

    if playerNode.position.y >= 180.0 &&
        playerNode.position.y < 6400.0 {

        backgroundNode.position =
            CGPoint(x: backgroundNode.position.x,
                    y: -((playerNode.position.y - 180.0)/8))

        backgroundStarsNode.position =
            CGPoint(x: backgroundStarsNode.position.x,
                    y: -((playerNode.position.y - 180.0)/6))

        backgroundPlanetNode.position =
            CGPoint(x: backgroundPlanetNode.position.x,
                    y: -((playerNode.position.y - 180.0)/8))

        foregroundNode.position =
            CGPoint(x: foregroundNode.position.x,
                    y: -(playerNode.position.y - 180.0))
    }
    else if playerNode.position.y > 7000.0 {

        gameOverWithResult(true)
    }
    else if playerNode.position.y + playerNode.size.height < 0.0 {

        gameOverWithResult(false)
    }

    removeOutOfSceneNodesWithName("BLACK_HOLE")
    removeOutOfSceneNodesWithName("POWER_UP_ORB")
}
```

The new update() method now calls the removeOutOfSceneNodesWithName() method at the end of every scene rendering, removing all unnecessary nodes. Make this change to the update() method and run the SuperSpaceMan game one last time. When you play the game this time, tap the screen until you're about to win the game and then stop tapping so that the playerNode starts to fall. This time as you fall, the passed-up orb and black hole nodes have been removed from the scene.

# Summary

In this chapter, you learned some SpriteKit best practices, including how to create your own subclasses of SKSpriteNode so that you can better reuse your nodes. You then moved on to changing your game to load all the sprites into a single texture. After that, you moved on to externalizing your game data. Finally, you pruned your node tree of all nodes that had fallen off the bottom of the screen.

In Chapter 10, you'll begin your journey into SceneKit. Have fun.

Part **II**

# Introduction to Scenekit

# Creating Your First SceneKit Project

In this chapter, you will dive right in and create your own game. For this game you'll make an homage to the classic Wolfenstein 3D game. First you'll learn how to programmatically create a scene and add nodes into the scene. After you have a basic understanding of these principles, you'll learn how to use the powerful SceneKit Editor in later chapters.

## SceneKit Primer

SceneKit is Apple's powerful 3D graphics framework that makes creating casual 3D games simple. By using the SceneKit API, you can create fully immersive 3D games without needing knowledge of OpenGL. SceneKit was first released for OS X Mountain Lion, and since the release of iOS 8, developers have created amazing 3D games with it. With the release of iOS 10 developers can now create 3D games for all Apples devices: iOS, tvOS, macOS, and watchOS.

SceneKit is used to create a *scene graph*, which contains a scene and a hierarchy of nodes, as shown in Figure 10-1. SceneKit uses these nodes to display scenes in a view and processes the scene graph using the graphics processing unit (GPU). This improves the performance of rendering the frames on the device.

© James Goodwill and Wesley Matlock 2017
J. Goodwill and W. Matlock, *Beginning Swift Games Development for iOS*,
DOI 10.1007/978-1-4842-2310-9_10

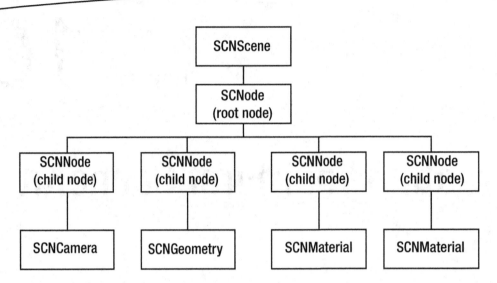

*Figure 10-1. Scene graph*

Apple has integrated SpriteKit within the SceneKit technology stack. This integration will allow you to use your SpriteKit knowledge to create your casual 3D game. Table 10-1 gives you an overview of the various classes and describes each of these SceneKit classes.

*Table 10-1. SceneKit Classes*

| Class | Description |
| --- | --- |
| SCNView | This view is used to display SceneKit objects. |
| SCNScene | A scene can be created programmatically or by using a 3D file from graphic tools. |
| SCNNode | This is the starting point to create a scene. |
| SCNCamera | This is the point of view for the scene. |
| SCNGeometry | This is a 3D object used to attach to a node. This also can use 3D files from graphic tools. |
| SCNMaterial | Material is used to describe how the surface of the node will be rendered. |
| SCNLight | This is a light source attached to a node to provide shading and lighting of the scene. |

# SceneKit Animation

SceneKit is also integrated with ImageKit and CoreAnimation, so you don't need any advanced knowledge of 3D programming. When you create scenes, you can create animations that transition elegantly between different values of the scene's properties.

SceneKit uses the SCNTransaction class to create an atomic run loop to combine all your implicit animation changes. These types of changes are ideally small atomic changes that occur almost immediately, and you can increase the duration. These types of animated properties automatically animate.

Because SceneKit is based on CoreAnimation, you can explicitly create animation objects and attach them to the animated scene. For this more complex animation, you subclass CAAnimation. After creating this subclass using key-value coding, set the animation parameters and attach them to the node or elements in the scene. The CAAnimation class is also able to use objects from third-party graphic authoring tools.

## What You Need to Know

SceneKit is a 3D-based API, so you should have a basic understanding of graphing concepts such as coordinate systems and 3D geometry.

- *Points*: In this context, a point is a position in a three-dimensional space.

- *Vectors*: You will use vectors mostly for directions.

- *Cartesian coordinate system*: This comprises two axes: the x-axis that extends along the horizontal plane and the y-axis that extends perpendicular to the x-axis.

- *Euclidean space*: This is simply the 3D coordinate system, with the addition of the z-axis that represents the depth of view.

- *Transformations*: Many operations do transformations, but for now you'll be dealing with operators that will be used for points and rotations. Think of this as transforming a point to a different point or applying a vector (direction) to the rotation of the object.

For more information on computer graphics programming, we suggest looking at *Geometric Algebra for Computer Graphics* by John Vince (Apress, 2008). By default, the camera, or user view angle, is along the z-axis (Figure 10-2).

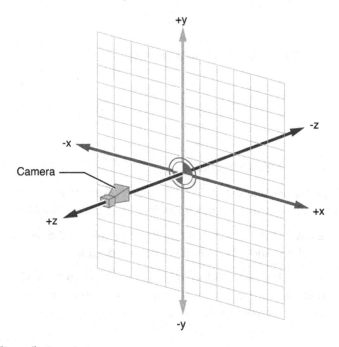

*Figure 10-2. SceneKit coordinate system*

# Creating the SceneKit Project

The best way to learn this is to simply dive in and start from scratch. You will create a game project using Swift as the language and SceneKit as the game technology. To create the project, open Xcode and complete the following steps:

1.  Select File ➤ New Project.

2.  Select Application from the iOS group.

3.  Select the Game icon. The Choose Template dialog should now look like Figure 10-3.

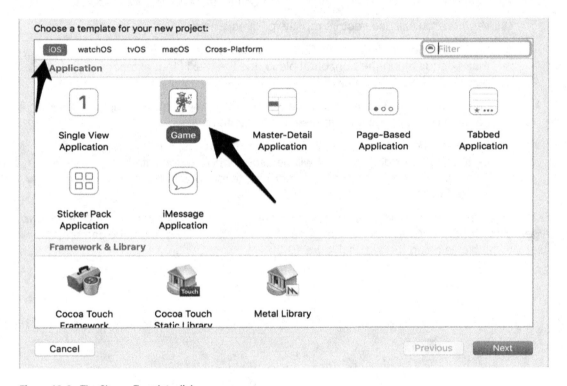

*Figure 10-3. The Choose Template dialog*

4.  To move on, click the Next button.

5.  Enter **SuperSpaceMan3D** for Product Name, **Apress** for Organization Name, and **com.apress** for Organization Identifier.

6.  Make sure Swift is the selected language, SceneKit is the selected game technology, and iPhone is the selected device.

7.  Before you click the Next button, take a look at Figure 10-4. If everything looks like this image, click the Next button and select a good place to store your project files.

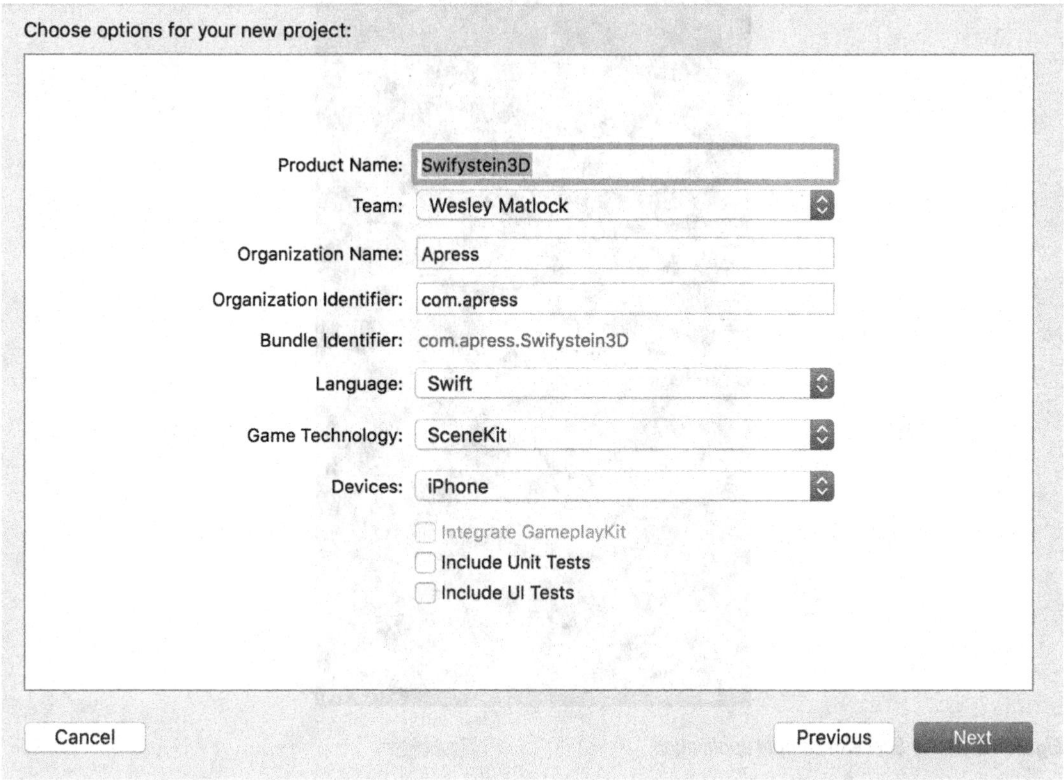

Choose options for your new project:

| | |
|---|---|
| Product Name: | Swifystein3D |
| Team: | Wesley Matlock |
| Organization Name: | Apress |
| Organization Identifier: | com.apress |
| Bundle Identifier: | com.apress.Swifystein3D |
| Language: | Swift |
| Game Technology: | SceneKit |
| Devices: | iPhone |

☐ Integrate GameplayKit
☐ Include Unit Tests
☐ Include UI Tests

Cancel                                    Previous        Next

*Figure 10-4.* *Choosing options for your project*

> **Note**   You're creating an iPhone-only game, but that's because this game lends itself better to the iPhone. Everything we cover in this book translates to any iOS device.

Once you click Next you'll be asked where you want to save the project. You now have a working SceneKit project, and you can click the Play button to see the default SceneKit game. If everything went OK, you'll see your new app running in the simulator. It doesn't do much yet, but you should see a spinning 3D rendition of a jet plane, similar to Figure 10-5.

*Figure 10-5. The SceneKit sample application*

# Wiring Up and Building a Scene

Now that you have a basic project and an understanding of SceneKit, it's time to actually learn how to put these classes together and create a game. Right now you have a project that's running the default Apple sample code. In this section, you'll remove that code and create a floor and the spaceman in his new environment.

# Swiftystein3D

Before you move on, let's get the project fully cleaned out so that you can start from scratch. Unlike the previous game that was in portrait orientation only, this time you will go with landscape orientation only, so you will need to change your target settings so they look like Figure 10-6.

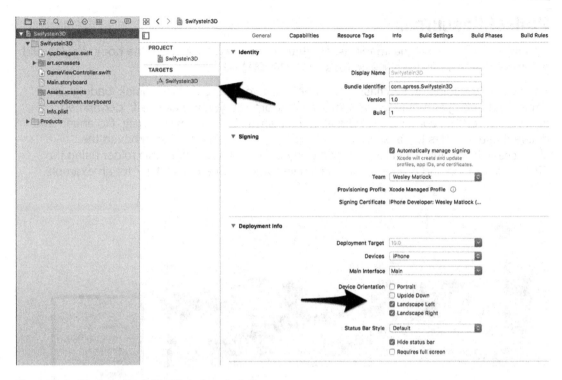

*Figure 10-6. The SuperSpaceMan3D device orientation*

The next thing to do is to replace the GameViewController.swift file's contents with the class in Listing 10-1. You want to override the viewDidLoad() method and create an empty SCNScene.

*Listing 10-1. GameViewController.swift: The GameViewController*

```
import UIKit
import QuartzCore
import SceneKit

class GameViewController: UIViewController {

    override func viewDidLoad() {
        super.viewDidLoad()

        // create a new scene
        view.SCNView()
    }
}
```

Now if you run the game, you'll see a blank screen, which is a great place for you to start the game.

# Project Resources

One thing you'll need is the image assets that will be used throughout the book. You should download these items from www.apress.com/97814823093.

Xcode uses the folder art.scnassests to optimize your 3D assets for quick loading and smooth rendering at runtime. If you look at your project, you will have a folder named art.scnassets that contains the default images ship.dea and texture.png. Go ahead and delete those two files because you won't use them. Now that you've removed the ship.dea and texture.png files, you can copy the game assets into this folder using the Finder application and dragging the images into Xcode. See Figure 10-7 for an example.

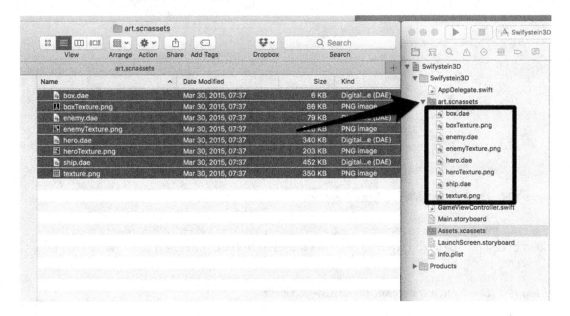

*Figure 10-7. Art assets*

Now that you have these files in the project, you need to add the static images to the project. This time you can simply drag the image from your folder in the Finder to the Xcode project and drop them into Xcode's image asset catalog: Images.xcassets. All the images that you'll be using for this game will be added at this time.

# Building the Scene

A good place to start is in the GameViewController class. You need to remove the temporary code in the viewDidLoad() method where you were creating an empty SCNScene:

```
override func viewDidLoad() {

  super.viewDidLoad()
}
```

In this class you'll create a class property that will be used to store the main scene variable. Right after the class declaration, go ahead and create the variable that will be used to store the main scene:

```
class GameViewController: UIViewController {

    var mainScene: SCNScene!
```

Using the best practices from the precious section, you'll use separate functions to create the objects for the game. This will allow you to understand what's going on and make it easier to refactor later if you want:

```
func createMainScene() -> SCNScene {

    let mainScene = SCNScene(named: "art.scnassets/hero.dae")
    return mainScene!
}
```

This method is small but powerful; this is where SceneKit's power starts to show. As you can see, you're loading a Collada file (.dae) that a 3D artist has provided you. Once you finish coding the scene, with just a few more lines of code you'll have the hero in his glorious 3D-ness.

Now let's add the scene that's being created to your view. In the viewDidLoad() method, you'll initialize the mainScene by calling your newly created function and then adding that scene to your GameViewController's view:

```
// create a new scene
mainScene = createMainScene()
let sceneView = self.view as! SCNView
sceneView.scene = mainScene

// Optional, but nice to be turned on during developement
sceneView.showsStatistics = true
sceneView.allowsCameraControl = true
```

This code will get the view, and then you add the scene to the view's scene. Since you're here, why not add showStatistics so you can see how well SceneKit handles 3D objects? You can also add allowsCameraControl = true so that you can manipulate the view using gestures. Pinching and zooming will zoom into the scene, and panning will allow you to pan around the scene.

Now you should be able to run the project and see the hero in full 3D, as shown in Figure 10-8. You can also spin him around and see him from all sides.

*Figure 10-8. Spaceman in 3D*

Before moving on, your GameViewController should look similar to Listing 10-2.

*Listing 10-2. GameViewController Class Setup*

```
class GameViewController: UIViewController {

    var mainScene: SCNScene!

    override func viewDidLoad() {
        super.viewDidLoad()

        // create a new scene
        mainScene = createMainScene()
        let sceneView = self.view as! SCNView
        sceneView.scene = mainScene

        // Optional, but nice to be turned on during developement
        sceneView.showsStatistics = true
        sceneView.allowsCameraControl = true

    }

    func createMainScene() -> SCNScene {

        let mainScene = SCNScene(named: "art.scnassets/hero.dae")
        return mainScene!
    }
}
```

Next you'll create a floor for the spaceman to walk on. In the GameViewController class, you'll create a new method that will create the floor node. Don't worry too much about an SCNNode—I discuss that in more detail in later chapters. However, nodes are the basic objects that are used in SceneKit scenes.

In the function declaration, you can see you'll return an SCNNode to the caller:

```
func createFloorNode() -> SCNNode {

}
```

Next you create a variable that will be the return SCNNode type, and you'll make the geometry of the node a SCNFloor. The SCNFloor is a special SceneKit class that creates an infinite plane. It's important to know that this plane will extend along the x- and z-coordinates, with the y-coordinate set to zero:

```
let floorNode = SCNNode()
floorNode.geometry = SCNFloor()
floorNode.geometry?.firstMaterial?.diffuse.contents = "Floor"

return floorNode
```

In this section of code, you set up the geometry for the floorNode. A node can have only one geometry assigned to it, so to create animated geometries, you'd create an empty node and add child nodes to it. For the floorNode, you won't be creating animated geometries, but that's something we touch on later in creating the game. You're also adding a material to the node, which in this case is the "Floor" image that you copied into the Assets.xcassets earlier in this chapter. You can simply think of the material as a color or image for now. Again, you'll dive deep into materials later.

You now have a method that will create a new SCNNode for the floor. Next you need to add it to your main scene so that you'll be able to see and interact with this node. Head back up to the createMainScene method, and after you create the main scene, add the following:

```
mainScene!.rootNode.addChildNode(createFloorNode())
```

Run the game now, and you'll notice that the spaceman is standing on a floor instead of in the middle of nowhere, as shown in Figure 10-9.

*Figure 10-9. Spaceman standing on the floor*

Run the game now, and you'll be able to move the view's perspective—in other words, a camera—around the object and see that you do have a 3D scene. You can do this because you set the camera control to `true`. Use the pinch-zoom and panning gestures to move around the scene. If you are running this in the simulator, notice the frames per second (fps) and see that it is never near 60 fps. On my simulator, it never gets above 20 fps. This time, run the game on your iPhone that has iOS 10 installed. Now when you move the camera around, you should see the fps stays closer to 60 fps. Does this mean your little iPhone is more powerful than your Mac? Probably not. The simulator is simply simulating the different devices to allow you as a developer to quickly test your code. However, when you run the game on an actual device, you can see the power of SceneKit. SceneKit is using the GPU to render the scene and nodes. This one reason why Apple recommends you always run the application on a device before submitting it to the App Store for approval. Before SceneKit was available, you had to use other third-party libraries or OpenGL in order to accomplish this. That could take more than several thousand lines of code to accomplish what you have done in less than 50 lines.

# Summary

Congratulations! You now have a simple 3D scene running. In this chapter, you learned some of the power that SceneKit provides. You created a project you will build upon. In Chapter 11, you'll examine what a scene graph is and how SceneKit works with a scene graph. You'll also start using some of SceneKit's built-in classes that will allow you to create the obstacles that will be used within the game.

# Chapter 11

# Scenes and Nodes

In this chapter, you'll learn how SceneKit uses the scene graph to render the objects in the scene. Once you have an understanding of the scene graph, you'll then see how to use the built-in models from SceneKit. You'll use the models to make obstacles in your game for the hero to avoid and for the enemy to hide behind.

## Scene Graph

Basically, the scene graphThe SCNScene is the base for a tree structure of the scene graph, as shown in Figure 11-1. In the early days of graphic programming, the scene graph was modeled with scene data, and its behavior was created procedurally, which usually led to a mess of code. Developers were unable to easily reuse your nodes or other objects through the application. A separation of concerns allows you to have a clean boundary between your scenes and how they're rendered. Figure 11-1 shows an example of how this looks.

© James Goodwill and Wesley Matlock 2017
J. Goodwill and W. Matlock, *Beginning Swift Games Development for iOS*,
DOI 10.1007/978-1-4842-2310-9_11

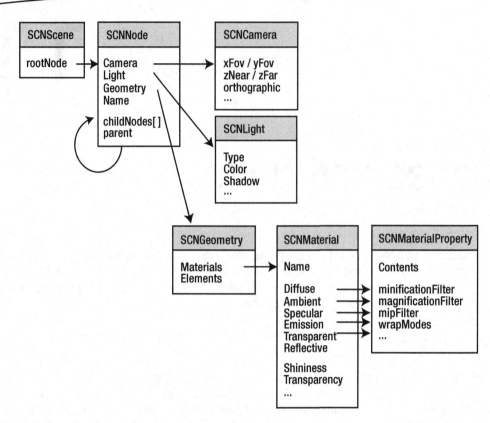

*Figure 11-1.  Scene graph example*

Every node in a scene has a parent except the topmost node—in other words, the root node. See Figure 11-2.

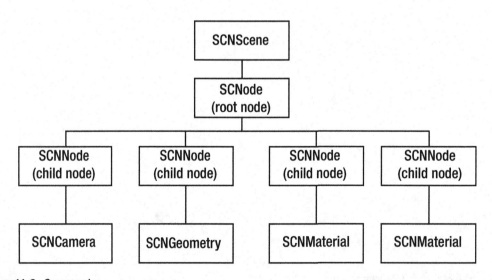

*Figure 11-2.  Scene nodes*

Nodes that contain other child nodes are considered *group nodes*. In Figure 11-2, you can see a parent node and several child nodes.

- Node trees (group nodes) are what appear in the scene. Node positions are defined in the coordinate system defined by its parent node.

- Leaf nodes are the ones that are actually rendered. These execute the animation and specify the material and lighting for the node tree.

# SceneKit's Built-in Model Classes

SceneKit provides almost all the primitive geometries that you'll need in order to create immersive games. You're going to use these simple geometries to create the first level of this game, so you can become familiar with these node types.

## SCNGeometry Objects

SceneKit provides several different geometries. When you create any of these geometries, the center is around its local coordinate system. In other words, if you create an SCNBox with the width, length, and height of 20.0, these will be along the x-, y-, and z-axes at 10.0 and –10.0.

Here is a list of the SceneKit primitive geometries types:

 SCNBox: This is a basic six-sided polyhedron with rectangles for faces. You'll also be able to create an SCNMaterial for each of these sides if you want.

 SCNCapsule: This is a cylinder that is capped at both ends by a hemisphere. You can define the hemisphere radius and the height.

 SCNCone: This is a geometric feature that has a circular base, and its sides taper at the center of the circle. You create an SCNCone by giving it a radius for the bottom and a height for the sides.

 SCNCylinder: To create an SCNCylinder, you give it a radius and a height.

 SCNFloor: This is an infinitely expanded plane along the x- and z-axes.

 SCNPlane: This is a one-sided surface that expands along the x- and y-axes.

SCNPyramid: When initializing an SCNPyramid, you give the height, width, and length for the pyramid.

 SCNSphere: This has the geometric shape of a globe. When instantiating an SCNSphere, you provide the radius to be used for the SCNSphere.

 SCNTorus: A torus is simply a circle around a coplanar axis, like a donut. You provide an inner radius and an outer radius for its circles.

 SCNTube: This is a tube or pipe. You give it an inner radius, an outer radius, and the height for the tube.

- SCNShape: This geometric shape is created from a Bezier path. SCNShape gives you the most control over the shape of your 3D object. 3D object.

- SCNText: You provide an NSString or NSAttributedString that is used to create a 3D object from this string.

As you can see, Apple has provided you with most of the shapes you'll need. You can combine these primitive shapes to create complex objects. However, for this game, you'll stick to the basic primitives for now. Let's get back into the code and start adding some obstacles for the spaceman to maneuver around in order to find the enemy.

# Adding Collectable Nodes

Now that you understand a little of the different type of geometric nodes we are going to use those as our "collectables" on this first simple level of your game.

Let's go ahead and create some geometric nodes that you'll use as collectable for your character to get. First you'll create a new file by either right-clicking the Swifystein3D folder and choosing New File or by choosing File ➤ New ➤ File. Either way you do it, you'll get to the File Template Selection, as shown in Figure 11-3.

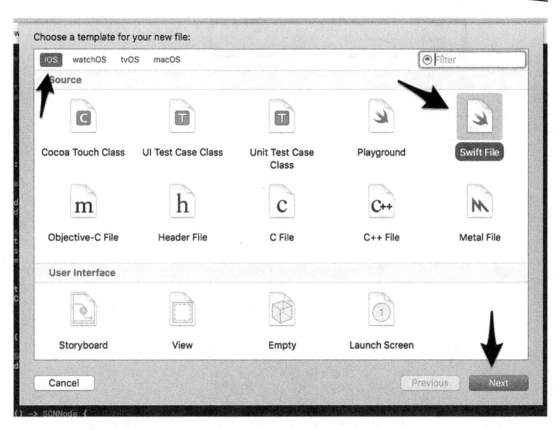

*Figure 11-3.  New file creation*

On the next screen name your file `Collectable.swift`, as shown in Figure 11-4.

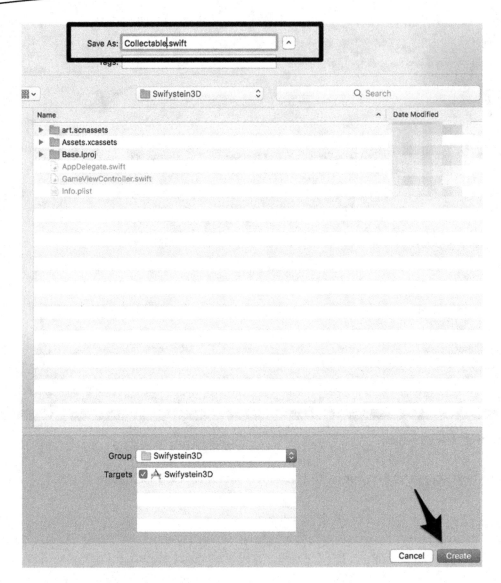

*Figure 11-4.  Creating a new Swift file*

Now you have a new blank file that you'll use to create the collectibles for the level of the game. The first thing you'll need to do is import SceneKit because you'll need to create SNNodes. You'll then create the Collectable class; once this is done your file should look like the code in Listing 11-1:

*Listing 11-1.  Collectable Class*

```
import Foundation
import SceneKit

class Collectable {

}
```

You'll do a few things differently in this class, in that you'll create class-level methods. If you are familiar with other languages, this is similar to static methods. Doing it this way is to expose you to another coding paradigm.

For your first collectable, let's create a PyramidNode method, as in Listing 11-2:

*Listing 11-2. Pyramid Node*

```
class func pyramidNode() -> SCNNode {

    // 1 Creating the SCNGeometry type
    let pyramid = SCNPyramid(width: 3.0, height: 6.0, length: 3.0)

    // 2 Create the node using the geometry type
    let pyramidNode = SCNNode(geometry: pyramid)
    pyramidNode.name = "pyramid"

    //3 Setting the node position
    let position = SCNVector3Make(30, 0, -40)
    pyramidNode.position = position

    return pyramidNode
}
```

Now let's go over this method and see what's going on:

1.  You first created a geometric object using the SCNPyramid SCNGeometry type. This allows you to easily manipulate the pyramid as you would any SCNNode.

2.  Next you created a SNNode based of the pyramid object. You also named this node pyramid. This naming of the node will help us later when you learn about collision detection later in the book.

3.  You now give the pyramidNode a position in the scene.

That's about if for creating a geometric node. The next thing you'll need to do is add this to the scene so you can actually see it when you run the game. Head to the GameViewController class. In this class find the createMainScene() method. You'll add in mainScene.rootNode.addChildNode(Collectable.pyramidNode()) after the mainScene.rootNode.addChildNode(createFloorNode()). It's important to add the new child node after the createFloorNode()

After adding the line of code, run the game. Now you see a pyramid slightly behind your hero, as shown in Figure 11-5.

*Figure 11-5. Pyramid node*

Well, there you have a pyramid in the middle of the screen. However, it isn't really nice to look at. Once thing we haven't discussed is the material of a node. You'll learn more about material and the SCNMaterial object in the next chapter, but you should at least add some color to this pyramid and the other collectables as you create them. Go back to the Collectible class and find the pyramidNode method. After the code line where you set the position, go ahead and add the following code:

```
// 4 Giving the node some color.
pyramidNode.geometry?.firstMaterial?.diffuse.contents = UIColor.blue
pyramidNode.geometry?.firstMaterial?.shininess = 1.0
```

What you're doing is setting the firstMaterial to the color blue. Remember, we'll go more into the diffuse and shininess in the next chapter. Right now you're just making the pyramidNode shine blue. Feel free to use any or the other UIColor defaults if you want. In fact, you'll create several more geometry type nodes with different colors here in a few minutes. Now when you run the game your pyramid will be blue, or whatever other color you set it to.

You now have some basic knowledge of how to create a primitive SceneKit geometric object. Now make sure you're in the Collectable class and using the same pattern in the pyramidNode create some more objects.

Let's continue to add another collectable and create a sphere node. Below the pyramidNode method add the code shown in Listing 11-3.

*Listing 11-3. Globe Node*

```
class func sphereNode() -> SCNNode {

    // 1 Creating the SCNGeometry type
    let sphere = SCNSphere(radius: 6.0)

    // 2 Create the node using the geometry type
    let sphereNode = SCNNode(geometry: sphere)
    sphereNode.name = "sphere"

    //3 Setting the node position
    let position  = SCNVector3Make(35, 0, -60)
    sphereNode.position = position

    // 4 Giving the node some color.
    sphereNode.geometry?.firstMaterial?.diffuse.contents = UIColor.red
    sphereNode.geometry?.firstMaterial?.shininess = 1.0

    return sphereNode
}
```

Now that you have this method, the next thing is to add it to the scene. Again go to the GameViewController and you'll add this to the mainScene. For now go ahead and comment out the addChildNode(Collectable.pyramidNode()) and below that add the following in the globe node:

```
// mainScene.rootNode.addChildNode(Collectable.pyramidNode())
mainScene.rootNode.addChildNode(Collectable.sphereNode())
```

Now when you run that game you'll have a red sphere floating on your floor, as seen in Figure 11-6. You may have to move and zoom the camera around in order to see the sphere up close.

*Figure 11-6. Sphere node*

We're sure you noticed that the sphere is going through your floor. This is not how we want the sphere to be. Several of these geometric types' axis is through the middle of the object. So, in this case, if you want it to float above the floor you'll need to adjust the y-axis to the radius of the sphere. In the `Collectable` class, change the `sphereNode.postion` to:
`let position = SCNVector3Make(35, 6, -50)`.

This time rerun the game and you'll see the sphere floating on top of the floor like we want it to be, as shown in Figure 11-7.

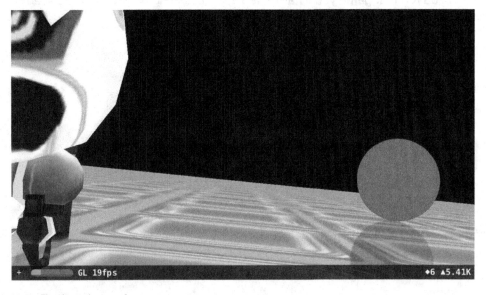

*Figure 11-7. Floating sphere node*

Feel free to adjust the position and see how the node moves around the scene.

You'll now add in several more geometric node types to the Collectable class. Listing 11-4 adds a box, tube, cylinder, and torus to the class.

*Listing 11-4. More Geometric Node Types for the Collectable Class*

```
class func boxNode() -> SCNNode {

    // 1 Creating the SCNGeometry type
    let box = SCNBox(width: 3, height: 3, length: 3, chamferRadius: 0)

    // 2 Create the node using the geometry type
    let boxNode = SCNNode(geometry: box)
    boxNode.name = "box"

    //3 Setting the node position
    let position  = SCNVector3Make(20, 1.5, -20)
    boxNode.position = position

    // 4 Giving the node some color.
    boxNode.geometry?.firstMaterial?.diffuse.contents = UIColor.brown
    boxNode.geometry?.firstMaterial?.shininess = 1.0

    return boxNode

}

class func tubeNode() -> SCNNode {

    // 1 Creating the SCNGeometry type
    let tube = SCNTube(innerRadius: 1, outerRadius: 1.5, height: 2.0)

    // 2 Create the node using the geometry type
    let tubeNode = SCNNode(geometry: tube)
    tubeNode.name = "tube"

    //3 Setting the node position
    let position  = SCNVector3Make(-10, 0.75, -75)
    tubeNode.position = position

    // 4 Giving the node some color.
    tubeNode.geometry?.firstMaterial?.diffuse.contents = UIColor.yellow
    tubeNode.geometry?.firstMaterial?.shininess = 1.0

    return tubeNode
}
```

```
class func cylinderNode() -> SCNNode {

    // 1 Creating the SCNGeometry type
    let cylinder = SCNCylinder(radius: 3, height: 8)

    // 2 Create the node using the geometry type
    let cylinderNode = SCNNode(geometry: cylinder)
    cylinderNode.name = "cylinder"

    //3 Setting the node position
    let position = SCNVector3Make(0, 4, -25)
    cylinderNode.position = position

    // 4 Giving the node some color.
    cylinderNode.geometry?.firstMaterial?.diffuse.contents = UIColor.green
    cylinderNode.geometry?.firstMaterial?.shininess = 1.0

    return cylinderNode
}

class func torusNode() -> SCNNode {

    // 1 Creating the SCNGeometry type
    let torus = SCNTorus(ringRadius: 7, pipeRadius: 2)

    // 2 Create the node using the geometry type
    let torusNode = SCNNode(geometry: torus)

    //3 Setting the node position
    let position =  SCNVector3Make(75, 1, -80)
    torusNode.position = position

    // 4 Giving the node some color.
    torusNode.geometry?.firstMaterial?.diffuse.contents = UIColor.orange
    torusNode.geometry?.firstMaterial?.shininess = 1.0

    return torusNode
}
```

After you've completed updating the `Collectable` class, don't forget you'll need to add them to the `mainScene` in the `GameViewController`:

```
let mainScene = SCNScene()
mainScene.rootNode.addChildNode(createFloorNode())
mainScene.rootNode.addChildNode(Collectable.pyramidNode())
mainScene.rootNode.addChildNode(Collectable.sphereNode())
mainScene.rootNode.addChildNode(Collectable.boxNode())
mainScene.rootNode.addChildNode(Collectable.tubeNode())
mainScene.rootNode.addChildNode(Collectable.cylinderNode())
mainScene.rootNode.addChildNode(Collectable.torusNode())
```

Run the game now, and it should look similar to Figure 11-8. You'll have to move the camera around (pan and zoom out) in order to see everything.

*Figure 11-8.  Geometric node layout — collectibles*

Right now they don't do much, and they're not all that interesting to see. Feel free to adjust the sizes and locations so that you can get a better understanding of how these variables change the object.

Take some time to adjust the position of these objects to make your own layout of these collectable. For the sample code, we put the objects in a large circle:

- *Pyramid position*: `let position = SCNVector3Make(0, 0, 200)`

- *Sphere position*: `let position = SCNVector3Make(0, 6, -200)`

- *Box position*: `let position = SCNVector3Make(200, 3.0, 0)`

- *Tube position*: `let position = SCNVector3Make(-200, 1.5, 0)`

- *Cylinder position*: `let position = SCNVector3Make(300, 8, 300)`

- *Torus position*: `let position = SCNVector3Make(-300, 0, 300)`

# Summary

In this chapter, you learned more about how SceneKit uses the tried-and-true scene graph to render objects. You also dove into the primitive objects that are provided to you in the SceneKit library. You'll expand on these primitives to create a simple yet interesting game as you progress through the book.

In Chapter 12, you'll learn how to manipulate the camera, which allows you to manipulate the point of view of the user. Another important aspect you'll examine closer is how lighting and materials can totally change the look and feel of your game.

# Lighting, Camera, and Material Effects in SceneKit

In this chapter, you will explore the camera and different views from the camera. You'll also learn about how the lighting of a scene works and the different type of lights that are available in SceneKit. Along with the lighting, you'll learn about how the object's material plays an important role in how the object is lit up and displayed to your user.

## SceneKit Camera Usage

The camera object is used to present scenes to the user from the camera location's point of view. You can use the camera object to set and adjust the field of view, near and distant visibility limits, and the focal length of the camera. Figure 12-1 shows you the main parameters of the field of view. These variables are as follows:

- xFOV: This is the angle at which the x-axis will be seen.

- yFOV: This is the angle at which the y-axis will be seen.

- zNear: This parameter is the minimal distance between the camera and the surface. Any object that is closer to the camera is not shown.

- zFar: This parameter is the maximum distance between the camera and the surface. Any object that is beyond this distance does not appear.

© James Goodwill and Wesley Matlock 2017
J. Goodwill and W. Matlock, *Beginning Swift Games Development for iOS*,
DOI 10.1007/978-1-4842-2310-9_12

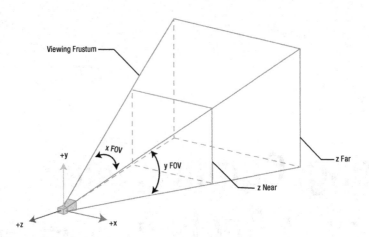

*Figure 12-1. Camera field of view diagram*

SceneKit provides you with two different types of cameras that you can use within your game.

- *Orthographic*: This type of camera represents the 3-deminsion environment into 2-deminsions. You won't be using this camera at this time.

- *Perspective*: This type of camera is used mostly in 3D first-person shooters, like the one you're writing.

The next piece of the code puzzle is to find the createMainScene() method. In this method, you will add a call to createHeroCamera(). You need to add this method call anywhere after the mainScene variable is initialized. You should have an unresolved error at this time; now you'll create the missing createHeroCamera() method, as shown in Listing 12-1.

*Listing 12-1. createHeroCamera() Method*

```
func createHeroCamera() {

    let cameraNode = mainScene.rootNode.childNode(withName: "mainCamera", recursively: true)

    cameraNode?.camera?.zFar = 500
    cameraNode?.position = SCNVector3(x: 50, y: 0, z: -20)
    cameraNode?.rotation = SCNVector4(x: 0, y: 0, z: 0, w: Float.pi/4 * 0.5)
    cameraNode?.eulerAngles = SCNVector3(x: -70, y: 0, z: 0) //Float(-M_PI_4*0.75))

    let heroNode = mainScene.rootNode.childNode(withName: "hero", recursively: true)
    heroNode?.addChildNode(cameraNode!)

    mainScene.rootNode.childNode(withName: "hero", recursively: true)?.
addChildNode(cameraNode!)
}
```

Let's go over this bit of code:

- You first initialize the cameraNode as a scene node (SCNNode()).

- After you have the node initialized, you initialize the camera parameter for the node.

- For this camera, you will need to set the zFar parameter. The zFar parameter is the maximum distance between the camera and the visible surface.

- The camera also needs a position; you'll set this position to be slightly behind and above the spaceman to start with. Later in the game development you'll adjust this position to follow the spaceman around the scene.

- You now need to set the rotation of the camera. Currently the camera is pointing straight ahead; however, because you put the camera slightly above your spaceman, you need to rotate it slightly down. This is exactly what setting the w: parameter in the SCNVector4 is doing.

Now that you've completed this method, your error should be gone. If you run your game now, you will now see the camera set to be above and behind the spaceman.

# Lighting Up the Scene

Ask any director or photographer, and one of the most important elements of a scene is lighting. You're in luck because SceneKit provides several types of lighting that you can manipulate to make your scene pop.

In SceneKit, you'll use the SCNLight object to create a light source in your scene. You'll set the light type to one of four different light types provided to you from SceneKit.

- SCNLightTypeAmbient: This light will illuminate your scene from all directions; the light's position or direction has no effect on the lighting of the scene.

Ambient

- SCNLightTypeOmni: This light will illuminate your scene from a certain point.

Omni

- SCNLightTypeDirectional: This light will illuminate all objects in your scene uniformly from the same direction.

Directional

- SCNLightTypeSpot: This light will illuminate your scene like a rock star!

Spot

So, these are the light types that you'll be able to use in your games. Note that the material of the object influences how the object is illuminated. Also, you'll have full control of the color of the light. SceneKit does have some "rules" it uses when updating a scene with lighting to make the scene display efficiently:

- Lighting affects only moving objects in your scene.

- SceneKit uses only up to eight light sources per node, so making more than this will be a waste. In fact, Apple recommends using no more than three lighting effects and a single ambient light.

We're sure you're ready to jump into some code. For your hero, you'll create a nice ambient light for the scene a spotlight so he is never in the dark.

To make things easy for you, you'll control all the lighting in the GameViewController for now. If you don't have the GameViewController open, open it up. You'll need to create a new class variable for the spotlight. At the top of the class, go ahead and create your new variable: var spotLight: SCNNode!. After you've created this variable, you can create the setupLighting() method, as in Listing 12-2.

*Listing 12-2. setupLighting() Method*

```
func setupLighting(scene:SCNScene) {

    let ambientLight = SCNNode()
    ambientLight.light = SCNLight()
    ambientLight.light!.type = SCNLight.LightType.ambient
    ambientLight.light!.color = UIColor.white
    scene.rootNode.addChildNode(ambientLight)

    let lightNode = SCNNode()
    lightNode.light = SCNLight()
    lightNode.light!.type = SCNLight.LightType.spot
    lightNode.light!.castsShadow = true
    lightNode.light!.color = UIColor(white: 0.8, alpha: 1.0)
```

```
lightNode.position = SCNVector3Make(0, 80, 30)
lightNode.rotation = SCNVector4Make(1, 0, 0, Float(-M_PI/2.8))
lightNode.light!.spotInnerAngle = 0
lightNode.light!.spotOuterAngle = 50
lightNode.light!.shadowColor = UIColor.black
lightNode.light!.zFar = 500
lightNode.light!.zNear = 50
scene.rootNode.addChildNode(lightNode)
}
```

First, you create SCNLight and SCNNode objects. As you can see, you'll set the type of light to the light object. A light type of SCNLightTypeAmbient doesn't need to set a direction, position, attenuation, spotlight angle, or shadows because an ambient light is for the entire scene.

Don't forget to call this method in the createMainScene() method, similar to setupLighting(mainScene).

# Materials

Now let's examine how SceneKit manages the visual attributes of your objects. SceneKit uses the SCNMaterial class to control the lighting and shading attributes for the geometry of your SCNNode.

SceneKit provides eight different properties you can use to set these attributes:

▪ *Diffuse*: Diffuse shading is the amount of light and color reflected in all directions.

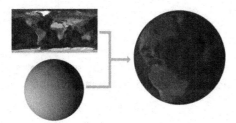

▪ *Ambient*: Ambient light is reflected in all points from the surface at a fixed intensity and fixed color. If there is no ambient light object in the scene, this attribute has no effect on the node.

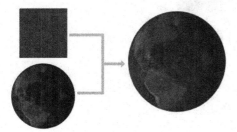

■ *Specular*: Specular is the light that is reflected straight to the user, similar to how a mirror reflects light. This is the bright spot of light that appears shiny on an object. This property is defaulted to black, which will cause the material to appear dull.

■ *Normal*: Normal lighting is a technique used to create lighting out of the surface of the material. Basically it tries to figure out the bumps and dents of the material to give more realistic lighting.

■ *Reflective*: Reflective lighting is a mirrored surface from the reflective environment. The surface will not actually reflect other objects in the scene.

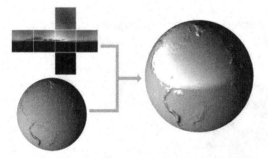

- *Emission*: Emission is the color that is emitted by the surface. By default, this property is set to black, which means no light is reflected. If you provide a color, that color will be reflected, and if you really want to get fancy, you can provide an image. SceneKit will use this image to provide the "glowing" effect based on the material.

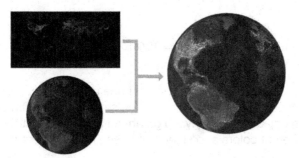

- *Transparent*: Transparent is the opacity of the material. This attribute is basically used to make parts of the material invisible.

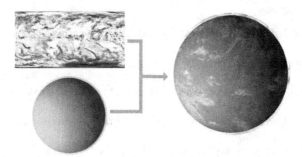

- *Multiply*: This attribute is computed after all the other attributes and adds a color to the material.

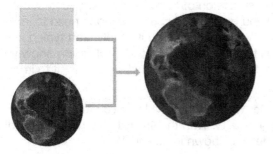

# Applying Materials to Your Obstacles

Now that you have a basic understanding of the attributes to the SCNMaterial, let's head over to the Collectible class and add some material to your collectibles.

First, make the PyramidNode a nice shade of blue, as in Listing 12-3.

*Listing 12-3. PyramidNode Material*

```
pyramidNode.geometry?.firstMaterial?.diffuse.contents = UIColor.blue
pyramidNode.geometry?.firstMaterial?.shininess = 1.0
```

In this game you're going to keep it simple and work with just one material. SceneKit provides easy access to this via the firstMaterial object. You set the diffuse contents to the color blue. You also want this object to be shiny, so go ahead and increase the shininess to 1. You can experiment with different colors and shininess to see how these attributes affect your PyramidNode.

Next up is your SphereNode. Listing 12-4 shows you how to add some items to make it look more like a miniature Earth.

*Listing 12-4. GlobeNode Lightening Enhancements*

```
sphereNode.geometry?.firstMaterial?.diffuse.contents = #imageLiteral(resourceName:
"earthDiffuse")
sphereNode.geometry?.firstMaterial?.ambient.contents = #imageLiteral(resourceName:
"earthAmbient")
sphereNode.geometry?.firstMaterial?.specular.contents = #imageLiteral(resourceName:
"earthSpecular")
sphereNode.geometry?.firstMaterial?.normal.contents = #imageLiteral(resourceName:
"earthNormal")
sphereNode.geometry?.firstMaterial?.diffuse.mipFilter = SCNFilterMode.linear
sphereNode.geometry?.firstMaterial?.shininess = 1.0
```

With the GlobeNode you're expanding on the NSMaterial and creating a more lifelike Earth. If you look at each of the JPG files, you'll see how these files affect the output from SceneKit and NSMaterial. The latest version of Xcode will allow you to use the image literal of the JPG file. So, when you type in this code you won't need to include the #imageLiteral(resourceName: "earthSpecular"). You'll simply start typing in the name of the image file: earthSpecular, for example, and Xcode will simply show you the image. Adding in the mipFilter to the diffuse property will allow SceneKit to improve the performance when rendering a texture image as a smaller size.

You'll now add some materials to the BoxNode. SceneKit allows you to apply an array to the materials, and it will apply this to the geometry. With the BoxNode, you'll apply six different materials, so you have six different sides, as shown in Listing 12-5.

*Listing 12-5. BoxNode Materials*

```
var materials = [SCNMaterial]()
let boxImage = "boxSide"
for index in 1...6 {
    let material = SCNMaterial()
    material.diffuse.contents = UIImage(named: boxImage + String(index))
    materials.append(material)
}

boxNode.geometry?.materials = materials
```

For the other obstacle types, add a color similar to how you did the PyramidNode. Listing 12-6 is the rest of the obstacles, so feel free to use different colors and images if you happen to have some images available.

*Listing 12-6. Remaining Obstacle Materials*

```
class func tubeNode() -> SCNNode {

    // 1 Creating the SCNGeometry type
    let tube = SCNTube(innerRadius: 8, outerRadius: 10.0, height: 10.0)

    // 2 Create the node using the geometry type
    let tubeNode = SCNNode(geometry: tube)
    tubeNode.name = "tube"

    //3 Setting the node position
    let position  = SCNVector3(-200, 1.5, 0)
    tubeNode.position = position

    // 4 Giving the node some color.
    tubeNode.geometry?.firstMaterial?.diffuse.contents = UIColor.yellow
    tubeNode.geometry?.firstMaterial?.shininess = 1.0

    return tubeNode
}

class func cylinderNode() -> SCNNode {

    // 1 Creating the SCNGeometry type
    let cylinder = SCNCylinder(radius: 6, height: 16)

    // 2 Create the node using the geometry type
    let cylinderNode = SCNNode(geometry: cylinder)
    cylinderNode.name = "cylinder"

    //3 Setting the node position
    let position = SCNVector3(300, 8, 300)
    cylinderNode.position = position
```

```
    // 4 Giving the node some color.
    cylinderNode.geometry?.firstMaterial?.diffuse.contents = UIColor.green
    cylinderNode.geometry?.firstMaterial?.shininess = 0.5

    return cylinderNode
}

class func torusNode() -> SCNNode {

    // 1 Creating the SCNGeometry type
    let torus = SCNTorus(ringRadius: 14, pipeRadius: 4)

    // 2 Create the node using the geometry type
    let torusNode = SCNNode(geometry: torus)

    //3 Setting the node position
    let position =  SCNVector3(-300, 3, -300)
    torusNode.position = position

    // 4 Giving the node some color.
    torusNode.geometry?.firstMaterial?.diffuse.contents = UIColor.orange
    torusNode.geometry?.firstMaterial?.shininess = 1.0

    return torusNode
}
```

# Summary

There was a lot in this chapter. You learned that SceneKit provides several different types of lighting. Spend some time experimenting with your code base and see how subtle changes in lighting can affect the playability of your game. Another learning experience was how SceneKit uses materials to make your objects more realistic or futuristic.

In Chapter 13, you'll examine how SceneKit moves objects around via animations.

# Render Loop, Physics, and Moving Around

So far in the game you have not moved the hero, and now you need to get him up on his feet and moving around. You're going to keep this simple and use a one-finger touch to move forward and two fingers to move back. To move left and right, you'll use the accelerometer. But where in the render loop do you actually put the code to move the hero around? Read on.

## What Is the Render Loop?

The render loop is SceneKit's game loop, and it's here that the game scene comes alive. The render loop happens once for each frame of the game scene that will allow you to perform game logic. The render loop has nine sections (see Figure 13-1) where SceneKit executes certain actions. SCNSceneRendererDelegate has five delegates where you can customize the game scene programmatically:

1. renderer(_:updateAtTime) is the first delegate to be called in the render loop. The delegate is where you would want to set up any logic that will be needed with in the loop.

2. During this phase of the loop, SceneKit runs the actions and animations of the nodes in the scene.

3. renderer(_:didApplyAnimationsAtTime:): After the animations have fun, this delegate is called by the view.

4. SceneKit's next action is to apply the physics to the nodes within the scene.

© James Goodwill and Wesley Matlock 2017
J. Goodwill and W. Matlock, *Beginning Swift Games Development for iOS*,
DOI 10.1007/978-1-4842-2310-9_13

5.   `renderer(_:didSimulatePhysicsAtTime:)`: After SceneKit has applied the physics, you have a chance to examine how the scene is progressing. This is where we will examine the movement and deal with any collisions that have occurred.

6.   SceneKit then evaluates the constraints of the view and nodes. These are items you'll be able to adjust that will allow SceneKit to automatically adjust the nodes in the view.

7.   `renderer(_:willRenderScene:atTime:)`: After SceneKit has evaluated the constraints and is about to render the scene, you have one last-minute delegate to make any adjustments.

8.   The view is rendered based on the scene graph.

9.   `renderer(_:willRenderScene:atTime:)`: This is the last and final delegate that is called before the loop starts again.

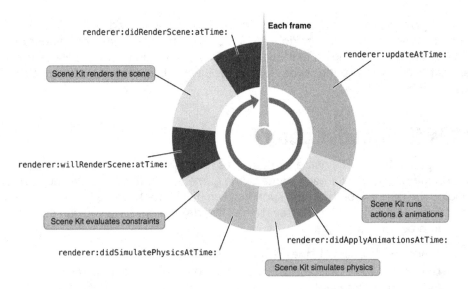

*Figure 13-1. SceneKit render cycle*

# GameView: Moving the Hero

Start by overriding the GameViewController's touchesBegan and touchesEnded methods. In Listing 13-1, you can see that you're overriding the touchesBegan method and the touchesEnded method.

*Listing 13-1. GameViewController.swift*

```swift
override func touchesBegan(_ touches: Set<UITouch>, with event: UIEvent?) {
    let taps = event?.allTouches
    touchCount = taps?.count
}

override func touchesEnded(_ touches: Set<UITouch>, with event: UIEvent?) {
    touchCount = 0
}
```

Here you're overriding the base function touchesBegan. You'll capture the touches that occur and assign them to the class variable touchCount. After the user releases the touch, you have to set the count to zero—otherwise, your poor hero would always be running. Now, go fix that error on the touchCount. At the top of the class add in the variable: var touchCount: Int?.

You'll use the render method in the GameViewController to read the touchCount variable in order to move the hero a direction based on how many touches occur during the render cycle of the render loop.

Now that you have the code in place to capture a touch, you need to put it somewhere where you can get the update from the scene. To do this, you'll use SCNSceneRendererDelegate and put your game logic into renderer. didSimulatePhysicsAtTime. In Figure 13-1, you can see this is one of the last times before the scene is drawn for you to make adjustments to the scene on a per-frame basis.

For you to receive these delegate notifications, you'll need to add SCNSceneRendererDelegate to your class declaration:

```swift
class GameViewController: UIViewController, SCNSceneRendererDelegate {
```

Now that you have the delegate, you need to assign it to an object that will handle the functions. In this case, you'll use the GameViewController self as the delegate. Add the following line of code in the viewDidLoad() function after the sceneView is declared:

```swift
sceneView.delegate = self
```

# Writing the Callback Delegate Function

Now you'll create the delegate function to get the callback from the SceneKit framework for every frame. Listing 13-2 shows the code you need in order to get this callback, and then you'll get the touchCount from the GameView in order to move the hero in one direction.

*Listing 13-2. Render Delegate Method*

```swift
func renderer(aRenderer: SCNSceneRenderer, didSimulatePhysicsAtTime time: TimeInterval) {

    let moveDistance = Float(10.0)
    let moveSpeed = TimeInterval(1.0)
    let heroNode = mainScene.rootNode.childNode(withName: "hero", recursively: true)
```

```
let currentX =  heroNode?.position.x
let currentY =  heroNode?.position.y
let currentZ =  heroNode?.position.z

if touchCount == 1 {
    let action = SCNAction.move(to: SCNVector3(currentX!, currentY!, currentZ! -
    moveDistance), duration: moveSpeed);
    heroNode?.runAction(action)

}
else if touchCount == 2 {
    let action = SCNAction.move(to: SCNVector3(currentX!, currentY!, currentZ! +
    moveDistance), duration: moveSpeed)
    heroNode?.runAction(action)
}
else if touchCount == 4 {
    let action = SCNAction.move(to: SCNVector3(0, 0, 0), duration: moveSpeed)
    heroNode?.runAction(action)
}

positionCameraWithSpaceman()
}
```

That was a lot of code, but you're doing several things in this function. You're also getting
an error about a missing method, positionCameraWithSpaceman—don't worry about that
right now because you'll add that method soon:

■  The first part of this code creates a few convenience variables to hold
   the current location of your spaceman as well as a couple of variables to
   control the speed and distance in which the spaceman will move during
   a render cycle.

■  Based on the touch count, you move him either forward the
   moveDistance value or backward the moveDistance value. Feel free to
   add some "Easter eggs" for your user to find, like that 11-touch gesture.

# Moving the Camera

Now that you have your spaceman moving, you need to move the camera with him to keep
him in the frame. You'll create the missing method positionCameraWithSpaceman, as in
Listing 13-3.

*Listing 13-3. positionCameraWithHero()*

```
func positionCameraWithSpaceman() {

    let heroNode =  mainScene.rootNode.childNode(withName: "hero", recursively: true)?.
    presentation
    let spacemanPosition = heroNode?.position
    let cameraDamping:Float = 0.3
```

```
let targetPosition = SCNVector3((spacemanPosition?.x)!, 30.0, (spacemanPosition?.z)! + 20.0)
let cameraNode = mainScene.rootNode.childNode(withName: "mainCamera", recursively: true)
var cameraPosition = cameraNode?.position

let cameraXPos = cameraPosition!.x * (1.0 - cameraDamping) +
targetPosition.x * cameraDamping
let cameraYPos = cameraPosition!.y * (1.0 - cameraDamping) +
targetPosition.y * cameraDamping
let cameraZPos = cameraPosition!.z * (1.0 - cameraDamping) +
targetPosition.z * cameraDamping
cameraPosition = SCNVector3(x: cameraXPos, y: cameraYPos, z: cameraZPos)

cameraNode?.position = cameraPosition!
}
```

- You get the hero node using the `presentationNode()` method so you can get his current position.

- Next, using a little math and the `SCNVector3` initializer, you position the camera above and behind the spaceman.

- While you're here, you'll light him up so he's the star of the game.

Now would be a good time to start up the game and check your progress. Once the game starts, notice that when you touch the screen, your hero moves forward some distance. Next, when you touch with two fingers, your hero moves backward a certain distance. This is great, but now you need to have your hero move left and right as well. For this you'll use the accelerometer to capture the tilting of the device.

Because this book is for SceneKit beginners, we won't go into too much detail about the CoreMotion framework; however, you'll use that framework to access the device's accelerometer. If you want to learn more about the CoreMotion framework, the Apple documents (https://developer.apple.com/library/content/navigation/) are a good place to start.

# Introducing CoreMotion Framework

The next step is to import the CoreMotion framework into your `GameViewController` class using `import CoreMotion`.

With `CoreMotion` imported, you can create another class-level variable that will store the CoreMotion manager. The reason you do this is because once you set up the CoreMotion manager, you'll create an `NSOperationQueue` that will run in the background and detect the movements from the accelerometer. After you have the class declaration, add `var motionManager: CMMotionManager`. Now you can create a method that will set up the accelerometer and capture the input from the accelerometer, as in Listing 13-4.

*Listing 13-4. setupAccelerometer Function*

```
func setupAccelerometer() {

    // Create the motion manager to receive the input
    let motionManager = CMMotionManager()
    if  motionManager.isAccelerometerAvailable {

        motionManager.accelerometerUpdateInterval = 1/60.0
        motionManager.startAccelerometerUpdates(to: OperationQueue()) {
            (data, error) in
            let heroNode =  self.mainScene.rootNode.childNode(withName: "hero",
            recursively: true)?.presentation

            // Get the current location.
            let currentX =  heroNode?.position.x
            let currentY =  heroNode?.position.y
            let currentZ =  heroNode?.position.z
            let threshold = 0.20
            // Moving right
            if (data?.acceleration.y)! < -threshold {

                let destinationX = (Float((data?.acceleration.y)!) * 10.0 +
                Float(currentX!))
                let destinationY = Float(currentY!)
                let destinationZ = Float(currentZ!)

                let action = SCNAction.move(to: SCNVector3(destinationX, destinationY,
                destinationZ), duration: 1)
                heroNode?.runAction(action)

            }
            else if (data?.acceleration.y)! > threshold {
                let destinationX = (Float((data?.acceleration.y)!) * 10.0 +
                Float(currentX!))
                let destinationY = Float(currentY!)
                let destinationZ = Float(currentZ!)

                let action = SCNAction.move(to: SCNVector3(destinationX, destinationY,
                destinationZ), duration: 1)
                heroNode?.runAction(action)

            }
        }
    }
}
```

Now that you've created this function, you can take a closer look at what is happening here.

The first thing you do is create a CMMotionManager. This is one of the entry points into the CoreMotion framework. Then you check to make sure you have an accelerometer. If you don't do this and run this code without the check, you'll get a crash whenever you try to use the manager. Also, some devices such as older iPods don't have accelerometers. Remember, your games and applications can run on just about any iOS device.

Now that you know there is an accelerometer, you'll want to set the update interval to be used. In some games, you may want to have the interval be slower or faster. For this game, you're going to get an update every 1/60th of a second. And because you're getting updated every 1/60th of a second, you don't want to tie up the main cycle of the game, so you'll create an update queue. This queue will take a closure and run this function every time the accelerometer update is called.

When the function is called, you create a few variables to store the current location of your hero. To keep things simple, you'll check to see whether the y-axis has changed a certain amount. A negative change indicates the user has tilted the device right, so you need to move the hero to the right; a positive change indicates the user has tilted the device left. Here you're using 0.20, but if you want a fine-grained adjustment, you can decrease that number.

Using this information, you simply create an animation for the hero to move a certain distance.

The only thing left now is to add the setupAccelerometer() call to your viewDidLoad() method in the GameViewController. Once you've added all that, it's another good time to run the game and see what you've accomplished.

When you have your hero moving by touching the device, tilt it to the left or right, and you'll see him move in that direction. There are some variables that you can adjust to have him move faster or slower. You should go back and modify the moveDistance in the render function to see how this affects the movement. Also, adjust the threshold in the setupAccelerometer function to see how the device response changes.

# Summary

In this chapter, you did a lot to get the spaceman moving. You also have the spaceman colliding with objects instead of going through them. In the next chapter, you'll examine the collision protocol to update the score and do a little animation on the collectible.

# Chapter 14

# Collision Detection

Now that you have the character moving around the screen, you will now need a way to identify when the hero finds a collectible. To do this you will use Collision Detection to know when the different nodes touch one another.

## Collision Detection

Now that you have the hero moving around and several collectibles for him to collect, you need to determine when your hero collides with one of them.

SceneKit uses the SCNPhysicsBody object to add physics simulations to a node. During the render of a scene, SceneKit prepares the frame in which it will perform physics calculations. These calculations include gravity, friction, and collisions with other nodes.

The SCNPhysicsBody class has a couple of properties that you need to set for each of your SCNNodes in order to detect the collisions. First thing you'll do is set the physics body to the hero node. Because the node is being loaded in the scene via the `let mainScene = SCNScene (named: "art.scnassets/hero.dae")` call in the `createMainScene` method, that's where you'll start. Before the `return` statement, add the following lines to that method:

```
let heroNode = mainScene.rootNode.childNode(withName: "hero", recursively: true)
        heroNode
heroNode?.physicsBody = SCNPhysicsBody(type: .dynamic, shape: nil)
```

The first thing you did was get the hero node from the main scene. Now you set the physics body to the node. SceneKit has three different types of physics bodies:

- *Static*: This type of physics body is unaffected by forces or collisions. You'll use this for the floor, obstacles, and walls because they will collide with objects, but they themselves won't move.

- *Dynamic*: This type of physics body is affected by forces or collisions. You'll use this type for the spaceman and enemy.

© James Goodwill and Wesley Matlock 2017
J. Goodwill and W. Matlock, *Beginning Swift Games Development for iOS*,
DOI 10.1007/978-1-4842-2310-9_14

■ *Kinematic*: This type is unaffected by forces or collisions but can cause collisions to occur within the physic world. You won't use this type, but it could be used for an invisible node that would represent the user's finger when touching an object.

Shape is the next parameter in the initializer. The shape defines the body for collision detection. In your calls, you'll set shape to nil, which will allow SceneKit to automatically create a physics shape based on the node's geometric property. If you want to have more control over the actual shape SceneKit uses for collision detection, then you can set it to a different shape. For your purpose, allowing SceneKit to define the shape will be enough for you.

Listing 14-1 gives you the physicsBody you'll need to set on all your nodes. So take your time and set each of the nodes at each of their locations. However, if you run the game right now you'll notice that our hero simply falls and vanishes below the floor. As you may have figured out, since the hero has a physical body now, it's interacting with the floor, which right now doesn't have a physical body, so gravity simply pulls the hero into the nether region.

Let's go ahead and fix that problem. In the createFloorNode() method, update the code before the return with the following statement:

```
floorNode.physicsBody = SCNPhysicsBody(type: .static, shape: nil)
```

Now when you run the game, the hero will stay on the floor and not fall through.

Next thing you need to do is add the physics body to all the collectibles in the Collectible class. This way the hero won't simply walk through them but instead will run into them. To make sure you're on the correct path, Listing 14-1 has the entire Collectible class as it should look after you've added in all the SCNPhysicsBodies.

*Listing 14-1. Collectible.swift with the SCNPhysicBody Set for All Objects*

```
//
//  Collectible.swift
//  Swifystein3D
//
//  Copyright © 2016 Apress. All rights reserved.
//

import Foundation
import SceneKit

class Collectible {

    class func pyramidNode() -> SCNNode {

        // 1 Creating the SCNGeometry type
        let pyramid = SCNPyramid(width: 3.0, height: 6.0, length: 3.0)

        // 2 Create the node using the geometry type
        let pyramidNode = SCNNode(geometry: pyramid)
        pyramidNode.name = "pyramid"
```

```
    //3 Setting the node position
    let position = SCNVector3(0, 0, 200)
    pyramidNode.position = position

    // 4 Giving the node some color.
    pyramidNode.geometry?.firstMaterial?.diffuse.contents = UIColor.blue
    pyramidNode.geometry?.firstMaterial?.shininess = 1.0

    pyramidNode.physicsBody = SCNPhysicsBody(type: .static, shape: nil)

    return pyramidNode
}

class func sphereNode() -> SCNNode {

    // 1 Creating the SCNGeometry type
    let sphere = SCNSphere(radius: 6.0)

    // 2 Create the node using the geometry type
    let sphereNode = SCNNode(geometry: sphere)
    sphereNode.name = "sphere"

    //3 Setting the node position
    let position  = SCNVector3(0, 6, -200)
    sphereNode.position = position

    // 4 Giving the node some color.
    sphereNode.geometry?.firstMaterial?.diffuse.contents = #imageLiteral(resourceName:
    "earthDiffuse")
    sphereNode.geometry?.firstMaterial?.ambient.contents = #imageLiteral(resourceName:
    "earthAmbient")
    sphereNode.geometry?.firstMaterial?.specular.contents = #imageLiteral(resourceName:
    "earthSpecular")
    sphereNode.geometry?.firstMaterial?.normal.contents = #imageLiteral(resourceName:
    "earthNormal")
    sphereNode.geometry?.firstMaterial?.diffuse.mipFilter = SCNFilterMode.linear
    sphereNode.geometry?.firstMaterial?.shininess = 1.0

    sphereNode.physicsBody = SCNPhysicsBody(type: .static, shape: nil)

    return sphereNode
}

class func boxNode() -> SCNNode {

    // 1 Creating the SCNGeometry type
    let box = SCNBox(width: 6, height: 6, length: 6, chamferRadius: 0)

    // 2 Create the node using the geometry type
    let boxNode = SCNNode(geometry: box)
    boxNode.name = "box"
```

```
        //3 Setting the node position
        let position  = SCNVector3(200, 3.0, 0)
        boxNode.position = position

        // 4 Giving the node some color.
        var materials = [SCNMaterial]()
        let boxImage = "boxSide"
        for index in 1...6 {
            let material = SCNMaterial()
            material.diffuse.contents = UIImage(named: boxImage + String(index))
            materials.append(material)
        }

        boxNode.geometry?.materials = materials
        boxNode.physicsBody = SCNPhysicsBody(type: .static, shape: nil)

        return boxNode

    }

    class func tubeNode() -> SCNNode {

        // 1 Creating the SCNGeometry type
        let tube = SCNTube(innerRadius: 8, outerRadius: 10.0, height: 10.0)

        // 2 Create the node using the geometry type
        let tubeNode = SCNNode(geometry: tube)
        tubeNode.name = "tube"

        //3 Setting the node position
        let position  = SCNVector3(-200, 1.5, 0)
        tubeNode.position = position

        // 4 Giving the node some color.
        tubeNode.geometry?.firstMaterial?.diffuse.contents = UIColor.yellow
        tubeNode.geometry?.firstMaterial?.shininess = 1.0
        tubeNode.physicsBody = SCNPhysicsBody(type: .static, shape: nil)

        return tubeNode
    }

    class func cylinderNode() -> SCNNode {

        // 1 Creating the SCNGeometry type
        let cylinder = SCNCylinder(radius: 6, height: 16)

        // 2 Create the node using the geometry type
        let cylinderNode = SCNNode(geometry: cylinder)
        cylinderNode.name = "cylinder"
```

```
        //3 Setting the node position
        let position = SCNVector3(300, 8, 300)
        cylinderNode.position = position

        // 4 Giving the node some color.
        cylinderNode.geometry?.firstMaterial?.diffuse.contents = UIColor.green
        cylinderNode.geometry?.firstMaterial?.shininess = 0.5

        cylinderNode.physicsBody = SCNPhysicsBody(type: .static, shape: nil)
        return cylinderNode
    }

    class func torusNode() -> SCNNode {

        // 1 Creating the SCNGeometry type
        let torus = SCNTorus(ringRadius: 14, pipeRadius: 4)

        // 2 Create the node using the geometry type
        let torusNode = SCNNode(geometry: torus)

        //3 Setting the node position
        let position =  SCNVector3(-300, 3, -300)
        torusNode.position = position

        // 4 Giving the node some color.
        torusNode.geometry?.firstMaterial?.diffuse.contents = UIColor.orange
        torusNode.geometry?.firstMaterial?.shininess = 1.0

        torusNode.physicsBody = SCNPhysicsBody(type: .static, shape: nil)

        return torusNode
    }
}
```

The next part of getting the collision detection working is to create the bit masks that will be used to determine when and if an object actually touches another one. Collision detection is based on using a bit mask that creates a table in order to determine whether two objects should collide. For this you'll create a new file called SharedConstants.swift, and you'll use this file to create the bit mask variables that will be used for all your objects. Listing 14-2 contains the code you need to add to this newly created file:

*Listing 14-2. SharedConstants.swift Contents for the Bit Mask*

```
let CollisionCategoryHero = 2
let CollisionCategoryCollectibleLowValue = 4
let CollisionCategoryCollectibleMidValue = 6
let CollisionCategoryCollectibleHighValue = 8
let CollisionCategoryFloor = 10
```

Now that you have the variables that you'll use for the bit mask, you'll need to again update all your nodes. As mentioned, these variables will be used to create a table to determine whether an object should collide with another.

SCNPhysicsBody has a couple of parameters that you'll set in order for the collision detection to work. The first of the two parameters is the category bitmask:

```
heroNode?.physicsBody?.categoryBitMask = CollisionCategoryHero
```

The second parameter to set is the collisionBitMask:

```
heroNode?.physicsBody?.collisionBitMask = CollisionCategoryCollectibleLowValue |
CollisionCategoryCollectibleMidValue | CollisionCategoryCollectibleHighValue
```

Basically, what you're doing the following: this node is the hero, and it will interact with the Collectible nodes of different values.

Listing 14-3 shows all the categoryBitMask and collisionBitMask values that you have to set on each of the nodes. Make sure you do this after the SCNPhysicsBody has been initialized and set on the node. It's also important that you initialize the physicsBody of the SCNode before it's added as a child to your scene.

*Listing 14-3. SCNPhysicsBody categoryBitMask and collisionBitMask*

```
// Add the following line to the GameViewController createMainScene() after the physicsBody
initialization:
heroNode?.physicsBody?.categoryBitMask = CollisionCategoryHero
heroNode?.physicsBody?.collisionBitMask = CollisionCategoryCollectibleLowValue |
CollisionCategoryCollectibleMidValue | CollisionCategoryCollectibleHighValue

//Add the following line to the Collectible pyramidNode() after the physicsBody initialization:
pyramidNode.physicsBody?.categoryBitMask = CollisionCategoryCollectibleLowValue
pyramidNode.physicsBody?.collisionBitMask = CollisionCategoryHero

//Add the following line to the Collectible sphereNode() after the physicsBody initialization:
globeNode.physicsBody?.categoryBitMask = CollisionCategoryCollectibleHighValue
globeNode.physicsBody?.collisionBitMask = CollisionCategoryHero

//Add the following line to the Collectible boxNode() after the physicsBody initialization:
boxNode.physicsBody?.categoryBitMask = CollisionCategoryCollectibleMidValue
boxNode.physicsBody?.collisionBitMask = CollisionCategoryHero

//Add the following line to the Collectible tubeNode() after the physicsBody initialization:
tubeNode.physicsBody?.categoryBitMask = CollisionCategoryCollectibleLowValue
tubeNode.physicsBody?.collisionBitMask = CollisionCategoryHero

//Add the following line to the Collectible cylinderNode() after the physicsBody initialization:
cylinderNode.physicsBody?.categoryBitMask = CollisionCategoryCollectibleHighValue
cylinderNode.physicsBody?.collisionBitMask = CollisionCategoryHero

//Add the following line to the Collectible torusNode() after the physicsBody initialization:
torusNode.physicsBody?.categoryBitMask = CollisionCategoryCollectibleMidValue
torusNode.physicsBody?.collisionBitMask = CollisionCategoryHero
```

Now it's time to check your work. Build and run the game and you should be able to move the spaceman around—only this time he can go through the nodes in the scene, he can go over some objects, and he is stopped by the walls.

Although that's great, you need a way for him to react to these collisions. Because you're making a hide-and-seek game, you'll want to know when you've found the enemy. In finding the enemy, you'll have to catch or collide with him. That's accomplished by using SCNPhysicsContactDelegate.

The first thing to do is tell your class that you want to receive the SCNPhysicsContactDelegate:

```
class GameViewController: UIViewController, SCNSceneRendererDelegate, SCNPhysicsContactDelegate {
```

In conjunction with this, you also need to set the delegate to a class that will respond to these collisions. In this case, you'll set the mainScene's contactDelegate to self so that the GameViewController can react to the collisions. In the *createMainScene()*, add this line before the return statement:

```
mainScene?.physicsWorld.contactDelegate = self
```

The SCNPhysicsContactDelegate has three protocols you can use, as shown in Listing 14-4.

*Listing 14-4. SCNPhysicsContact Protocols*

```
func physicsWorld(_ world: SCNPhysicsWorld, didBegin contact: SCNPhysicsContact) {
    print("didBeginContact")
}

func physicsWorld(_ world: SCNPhysicsWorld, didEnd contact: SCNPhysicsContact) {
    print("didEndContact")
}

func physicsWorld(_ world: SCNPhysicsWorld, didUpdate contact: SCNPhysicsContact) {
    print("didUpdateContact")
}
```

You should add Listing 14-4 to your GameViewController. This time when you run your game, you'll get the notifications when your spaceman moves around and interacts with the environment. For this game, though, you'll be using only the didBeginContact protocol. It will be at this time that you check to see whether the contact object has the node for the hero and the node for the collectible. To do this, you'll keep things simple and check nodeB for what type of contact was made in Listing 14-5.

*Listing 14-5. SCNPhysicsWorld didBeginContact Protocol*

```
func physicsWorld(_ world: SCNPhysicsWorld, didBegin contact: SCNPhysicsContact) {

    switch contact.nodeB.physicsBody!.collisionBitMask {

    case CollisionCategorycollectibleLowValue:
        print("Hit a low value collectible.")
```

```
case CollisionCategorycollectibleMidValue:
    print("Hit a mid value collectible.")

case CollisionCategorycollectibleHighValue:
    print("Hit a high value collectible.")

default:
    print("Hit something other than a collectible.")
  }
}
```

Now you're just going to print a line when you hit either the enemy or an obstacle. So, run your game now and move the spaceman around the playing field. As you keep an eye on the console logs, note that when you run into an obstacle or the enemy, the appropriate line is output.

# Summary

In this chapter, you did a lot to get the spaceman moving. You also now have the spaceman colliding with objects instead of going through them. At this point, you're almost finished with the hide-and-seek game.

In Chapter 15 you'll use this collision protocol to update the score. This scoreboard that you'll create will be in a SpriteKit view. This way, you can see how to combine a SpriteKit view with in a SceneKit scene.

# SceneKit Interaction with SpriteKit

In the previous chapters, you've worked within the SceneKit paradigm; however, Apple has created a way for you to add a 2D scene to overlay on your 3D scenes. In this chapter, you'll add a 2D scene that will be used for your timer so it can track how long it will take you and your friends to find and capture the enemy.

## SpriteKit Integration

SceneKit gives you a property to add a SpriteKit scene:

```
var overlaySKScene: SKScene! { get set }
```

This property can render a 2D scene that overlays the SceneKit scene. To provide better performance, SceneKit and SpriteKit use the same OpenGL context and resources to render the scene.

For this game, you'll add a scoreboard to the top of the scene. To get started, create a new Swift file and name it `GameOverlay.swift`.

Now that you have the file created, you need to import both SceneKit and SpriteKit:

```
import SceneKit
import SpriteKit

class GameOverlay: SKScene {

}
```

Your class should look similar to the preceding code snippet. Your `GameOverlay` class is a subclass from the `SKScene`, which should look familiar from previous chapters. For this class, you'll add a node for the score and another one to keep track of the player's lives.

© James Goodwill and Wesley Matlock 2017
J. Goodwill and W. Matlock, *Beginning Swift Games Development for iOS*,
DOI 10.1007/978-1-4842-2310-9_15

The first part you'll need to do is make one variable to hold the SKLabelNode object. Because you'll be using the time interval from Date, you need to create a NumberFormatter:

```
var timerNode: SKLabelNode!
var scoreNode: SKLabelNode!
var timerFormat: NumberFormatter!
```

Now that you have some variables, you'll need to initialize them before you use them. Listing 15-1 shows you the overridden init(size: CGSize) function.

*Listing 15-1. GameView.init*

```
override init(size: CGSize) {
    super.init(size: size)

    anchorPoint = CGPoint(x: 0.5, y: 0.5)
    scaleMode = .resizeFill

    timerNode = SKLabelNode(fontNamed: "AvenirNext-Bold")
    timerNode.text = "Time: 0.0"

    timerNode.fontColor = .red
    timerNode.horizontalAlignmentMode = .left
    timerNode.verticalAlignmentMode = .bottom
    timerNode.position = CGPoint(x: -size.width/2 + 20, y: size.height/2 - 40)
    timerNode.name = "timer"
    addChild(timerNode)

    timerFormat = NumberFormatter()
    timerFormat.numberStyle = .decimal
    timerFormat.minimumFractionDigits = 1
    timerFormat.maximumFractionDigits = 1
}
```

In this initializer function, you're doing a few things that you should stop and look at before moving on. This first part is creating the SKLabelNode that will be used to show the timer counting up. You can change the font and color, if you want, to something that would suit your needs better; however, the red with Copperplate looks pretty decent in this game.

Following the SKLabelNode setup is the NumberFomatter setup section. The NumberFomatter allows you to use numbers to be represented as String text. You'll have a maximum and minimum of one fraction digit. This will allow you to show the timer within 1/10th of a second. Don't forget, you'll also need to override the required initializer, as in Listing 15-2.

*Listing 15-2. Required Initializer*

```
required init?(coder aDecoder: NSCoder) {
    fatalError("init(coder:) has not been implemented")
}
```

When your game starts, you'll need start the timer so the user knows how fast he gets to the enemy. To do that, you'll create a function that will start the timer, and it will update your SKLabelNode for the player. Listing 15-3 shows the startTimer() for this purpose.

*Listing 15-3.  GameOverlay.startTimer()*

```
func startTimer() {
  let startTime = NSDate.timeIntervalSinceReferenceDate
  let timerNode = childNode(withName: "timer") as! SKLabelNode

  let timerAction = SKAction.run({ () -> Void in
      let now = NSDate.timeIntervalSinceReferenceDate
      let elapsedTime = TimeInterval( now - startTime )
      let tempString = String(format: "%@",  self.timerFormat.string(from: NSNumber
      (value: elapsedTime))!)
      timerNode.text = "Time: " + tempString
  })
  let startDelay = SKAction.wait(forDuration: 0.5)
  let timerDelay = SKAction.sequence([timerAction, startDelay])
  let timer = SKAction.repeatForever(timerDelay)
  timerNode.run(timer, withKey: "timerAction")
}
```

The next function you need to add to the GameOverlay class is to stop the timer when you have collected all the collectibles. If you look at Listing 15-4, you can see it's pretty simple. You'll get the node that you named timer in the start function and then stop the action with a new function called: timerAction.

*Listing 15-4.  GameOverlay.stopTimer*

```
func stopTimer() {
    let timerNode =  childNode(withName: "timer") as! SKLabelNode
    timerNode.removeAction(forKey: "timerAction")
}
```

You have your GameOverlay class completed. Now you need to update the GameViewController to use this class and place it over your 3D SceneKit scene.

# Hooking Up the Controller to the Overlay

You have the GameOverlay class complete, so now it's time to connect it to the GameViewController. First, you want to create a class-level variable that you'll use to get access to the GameOverlay class. Doing so, you'll easily be able to call the methods to start the timer. You'll also need to create a Boolean that will be used to keep track of the starting of the game:

```
var gameOverlay: GameOverlay!
gameStarted = false
```

In the GameViewController viewDidLoad function, add this GameOverlay to the SCNScene. Doing so will allow the SceneKit framework to overlay your GameOverlay onto the current scene:

```
sceneView.overlaySKScene = GameOverlay(size:view.frame.size)
gameOverlay =  sceneView.overlaySKScene as! GameOverlay
```

Right now is a good time to run your game and see the overlay timer on top of the scene you've been working on. Once you run the game, you should have a scene similar to Figure 15-1.

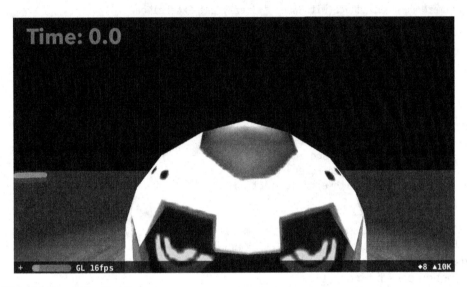

*Figure 15-1. Overlay scene with a timer*

Now that you have the overlay, you need to start the timer when the user begins to move the spaceman. Because you'll be using the `touchCount` in the `sceneView` to start the timer, you'll want to also make sure your player hasn't already started the game—otherwise, the timer will always reset itself with every touch. After the `GameViewController` class definition, you'll add another variable that will be used as a flag for when the game starts, and you'll initialize it to false: `var gameStarted = false`.

Now when your player starts the game, you'll set this to true and then back to false at the end of the game. To accomplish that, you'll need to add some logic into the `didSimulatePhysicsAtTime` function in the `GameViewController`:

```
func renderer(aRenderer: SCNSceneRenderer, didSimulatePhysicsAtTime time: TimeInterval) {
```

In this function, you'll add Listing 15-5 at the top of the function. This checks to see whether the user has touched the screen, and if so it starts the timer and sets the `gameStarted` flag. You'll use this flag later in the code.

*Listing 15-5. Start the Timer in the didSimulatePhysicsAtTime Protocol*

```
if touchCount > 0 && !gameStarted {
    gameOverlay.startTimer()
    gameStarted = true
}
```

This time when you run the game, you'll notice the timer start running when you touch the device, as in Figure 15-2.

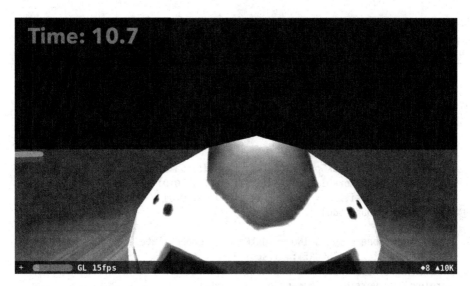

*Figure 15-2. Timer running*

The last thing you need to do for the timer is to call the stopTimer() method when you've collected all the collectibles. The best place for that will be in the SCNPhysicsWorld didBeginContact protocol. You'll do a check after the switch statement to see if you have a score over a certain amount—in this case, 50 points:

```
if gameOverlay.score >= 50 {
    gameOverlay.stopTimer()
}
```

This time when you run the game and maneuver the hero around collecting collectibles, the timer will stop when you've achieved the score needed to move to the next level, as well as the time it took you to get to this amount.

## "Game Over" Screen

You have a working game now, but wouldn't it be nice to have a "Game Over" screen to show your time and score and be able to restart the game? You'll create another view that will update the sceneView.overlaySKScene when the hero achieves the score.

Create a new Swift file called GameOverView.swift just as you've created in the past. The GameOverView will look familiar—Listing 15-6 has the code you need to put into the GameOverView class.

*Listing 15-6.  GameOverView*

```
import SpriteKit

class GameOverView: SKScene {

    required init?(coder aDecoder: NSCoder) {
        super.init(coder: aDecoder)
    }

    init(size: CGSize, score: String) {
        super.init(size: size)

        backgroundColor = .red
        let backgroundNode = SKSpriteNode(imageNamed: "GameOverBackground")
        backgroundNode.anchorPoint = CGPoint(x: 0.5, y: 0.0)
        backgroundNode.position = CGPoint(x: 160.0, y: 0.0)
        addChild(backgroundNode)

        let scoreTextNode = SKLabelNode(fontNamed: "Copperplate")
        scoreTextNode.text = "SCORE :  \(score)"
        scoreTextNode.horizontalAlignmentMode = .center
        scoreTextNode.verticalAlignmentMode = .center
        scoreTextNode.fontSize = 20
        scoreTextNode.fontColor = .white
        scoreTextNode.position = CGPoint(x: size.width / 2.0, y: size.height - 75.0)
        addChild(scoreTextNode)

        let tryAgainText = SKLabelNode(fontNamed: "Copperplate")
        tryAgainText.text = "TAP ANYWHERE TO PLAY AGAIN!"
        tryAgainText.horizontalAlignmentMode = .center
        tryAgainText.verticalAlignmentMode = .center
        tryAgainText.fontSize = 20
        tryAgainText.fontColor = .white
        tryAgainText.position = CGPoint(x: size.width / 2.0, y: size.height - 200)
        addChild(tryAgainText)
    }
}
```

Listing 15-7 shows the updated didBeginContact method. The player makes contact with a collectible, and the score is updated. Next, the time is stopped if the player has achieved the score for the level. If this happens, you will then display the "game over" view to the user.

*Listing 15-7.  Score Check and Display Game Over Scene*

```
if gameOverlay.score >= 50 {
    gameOverlay.stopTimer()
    sceneView.overlaySKScene = GameOverView(size: view.bounds.size, score:
    String(gameOverlay.score))
}
```

Now when you run your game and you get to the enemy, the player will be shown a "game over" view and their time.

There's one other item you need to deal with, and that's to update the sceneView. overlaySKScene to the original timer screen. To restart the player, just touch anywhere on the screen in order to restart the game, as shown in Figure 15-3.

*Figure 15-3. "Game over" screen*

# Summary

Now you have an overlay SpriteKit scene that has a timer, and you're randomly placing the objects in the scene. You can expand on this overlay scene and add more SpriteKit features as you choose to for your games.

You now have a simple game that has explored Apple's SceneKit library. You've learned what a scene graph is and how SceneKit uses this graph to display 3D objects while using the GPU on the device. Try running this game in the simulator instead of on the device, and you'll see how much the GPU improves performance.

# Chapter 16

# SceneKit Editor

Now that you have a basic understanding of how SceneKit works, you can now use the render loop to create, control, and animate SCNodes. In previous chapters, you've been using code to manipulate those objects. In this chapter, you'll learn how to do the same thing in the SceneKit Editor.

## The SceneKit Scene

If you haven't downloaded the source code from the Apress website, you'll have to for this section. The Xcode project contains all the graphical assets you'll need to follow along with this chapter. Download it from www.apress.com/97814823093.

Open the Swiftystein3D project if you don't have it open already. First thing you'll do is add in a new SceneKit file from the Resources section of the Add New file. Now go ahead and right-click the project to add a file to the project, as in Figure 16-1.

© James Goodwill and Wesley Matlock 2017
J. Goodwill and W. Matlock, *Beginning Swift Games Development for iOS*,
DOI 10.1007/978-1-4842-2310-9_16

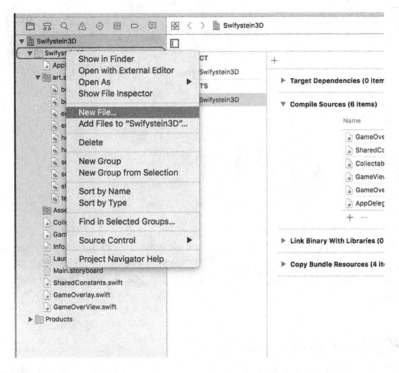

*Figure 16-1. Adding a new file*

After you've selected New File, the next screen you'll see is similar to Figure 16-2. You may have to scroll down in order to see the SceneKit Scene Resource.

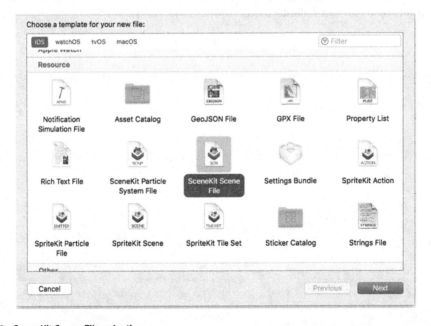

*Figure 16-2. SceneKit Scene File selection*

Once you've selected the SceneKit Scene File, you will this file Level1.scn.

You now have a blank Level1 scene that you'll use to create a simple scene like the simple scene you created programmatically. Figure 16-3 shows the entire SceneKit Editor that we'll go over.

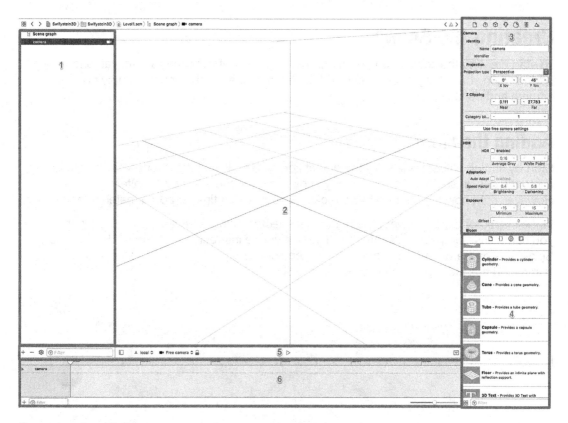

*Figure 16-3. SceneKit Editor*

Here's an overview of the SceneKit Editor:

1. *Scene graph*: This section has every node/element in the scene. This tree is where you can control the child-parent relationship to the nodes.

2. *Design section*: This section is where you'll drag and drop your objects from the object library section (4). You'll have a visual representation of all your nodes so you can easily move items around and change their properties.

3. *Inspectors/properties*: As you select objects in the design section, you'll have many properties that you can adjust and control. As you make these adjustments, you'll see right away visually what will happen.

4.  *Object library*: This section has all the objects that you can add to the scene. You simply drag and drop the object you want and then adjust in the inspector/properties.

5.  *Actions*: This section allows you to add actions to a selected node.

# Creating the Scene

To start creating the scene, you first need to delete the default camera that was originally added when you initially added the new file. In the scene graph section, simply click the camera and delete it.

# Adding the Floor

Start by adding a floor node from the object library. Simply find the floor and drag and drop it into the design section. As you already know, a floor node will grow infinitely automatically. However, right now the floor is simply a clear object, so it's time to add a material to the floor.

In the inspector section, select the material inspector. This shows all the properties that you can adjust for the node's material. The one you're interested in is the Diffuse property. Select this property and scroll through your choices to sceneFloor.png. Once you've completed this step, your screen should look like Figure 16-4.

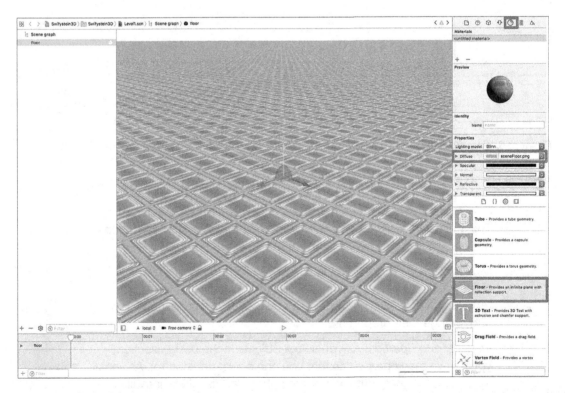

*Figure 16-4. Flood node scene*

# Adding the Hero

One very powerful thing you can do with in the Scene Editor is simply drag and drop other scenes, including DAE files, onto this level scene. This capability allows your graphic designer to create beautiful objects that you can use in your game level.

You've used hero.dea in previous chapters when you programmatically created the scene. This time you'll drag and drop that file on to the Level1 design section of the Editor. When you drag and drop a new scene into the current scene, you're actually creating a reference to the original file. By creating a reference if you have an object in multiple scenes (Levels, in this case), you would only need to update the original file, and then all the other references would be updated. For example, if you decided you wanted to change the textures of the hero, you would only have to make those changes on the Hero.dea file. Then anywhere that file is referenced it would be updated. Figure 16-5 shows what your scene should resemble.

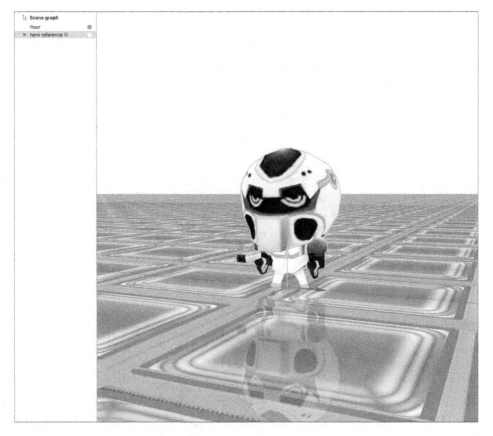

*Figure 16-5.  Hero node placed into scene*

If your placement of the hero node doesn't look exactly like Figure 16-5, don't worry.

Now that you have a couple of nodes, let's go over some of the inspector properties that you can use to manipulate the node. Make sure you've selected the hero reference node. Figure 16-6 shows the node inspector, and one of the properties you can adjust is the position of the node, the scale, and the angle at which the node is located. As you can see, there are several other properties at your disposal. Because we're keeping things simple, we'll leave most of the at the default for now. However, feel free to explore each of these properties—that's the beauty of the SceneKit Editor.

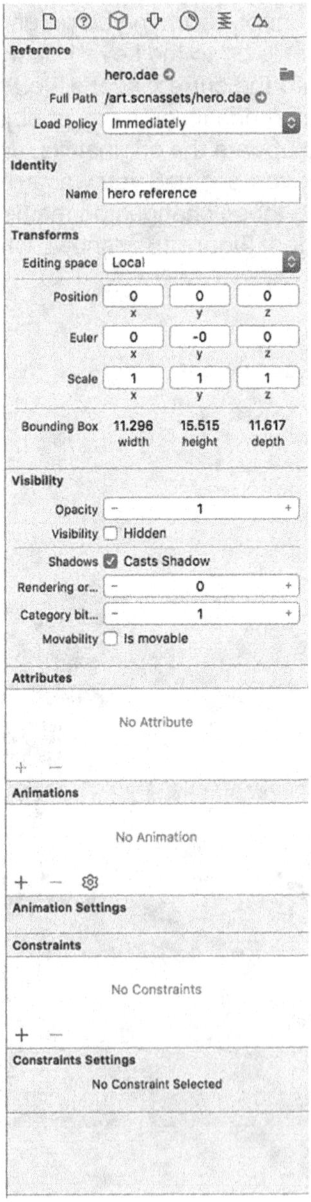

Figure 16-6. Node inspector

## Adding in the Camera

Now that you have the hero in place, you need to add a camera so that when you play the game you can follow the hero around. Drag the camera node from the object library into the scene graph. Don't worry about where the camera is placed—you'll make the adjustments in the node inspector and change the position and Euler angle so that the camera is right above and behind the hero. Figure 16-7 shows the settings to make to the camera.

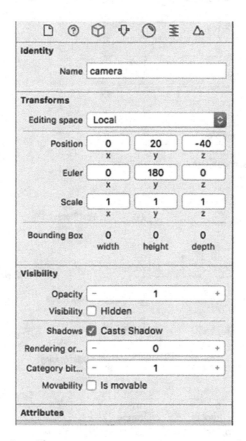

*Figure 16-7.* *Camera node inspector settings*

Now we'll go over the attribute inspector shown in Figure 16-8, and you can see some of the new and exciting attributes that Apple introduced into iOS 10 SceneKit.

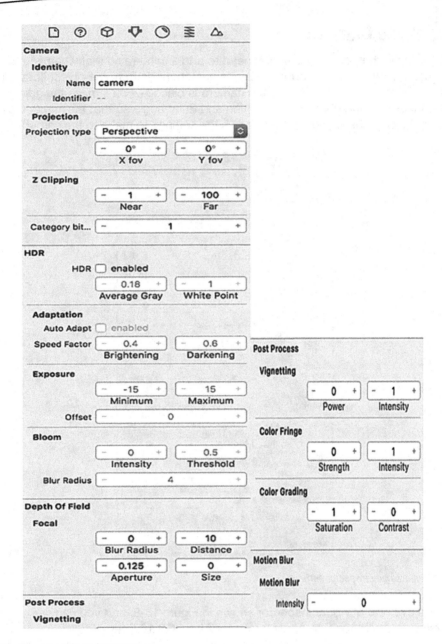

*Figure 16-8.* *Camera attribute inspector*

The properties we will explore are as follows:

- *HDR*: You can now enable the High Dynamic Range technique for your scene. This produces a greater dynamic range of lighting. Average Gray is the middle of the lighting tone used in the mapping of the light curve. White Point is the higher level of lighting tone used in the mapping of the light curve.

- *Adaption*: This is an interesting effect that controls the way the player's eyes adjust when the lightening changes from light to dark and vice versa. Think of this as when your scene transitions from inside a dark dungeon to the bright outside.

- *Exposure*: Basically, the darkness and lightness of the scene.

- *Bloom*: This is that haziness you see around a brightly light area.

- *Depth of Field*: These items have been around and reviewed in previous sections.

- *Post Processing*: More newness attributes introduced in iOS 10:

    - *Vignetting*: Allows you to control the lightening around the edges of the scene

    - *Color Fringe*: Gives your scene some color mixing around nodes

    - *Color Grading*: Allows you to enhance the overall color saturation of the rendered scene

- *Motion Blur*: This property adds the blurring effect to all objects that are in motion.

Once you have the camera set up, Figure 16-9 shows how your scene should look now.

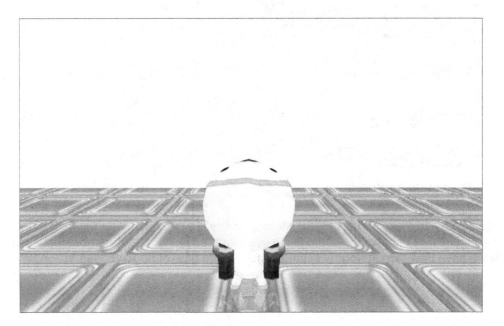

*Figure 16-9.* *Current scene with camera*

## Adding in Nodes

Now you can start adding in the collectible nodes just as you did programmatically in earlier chapters. In the object library, simply drag and drop in a few of the different types of nodes. For example, drag out a pyramid, sphere, capsule, and any other type you want to use.

Figure 16-10 depicts dragging out the sphere node and setting the location manually in the inspector. This is something you'll have to do in order to fine-tune your placement of the nodes.

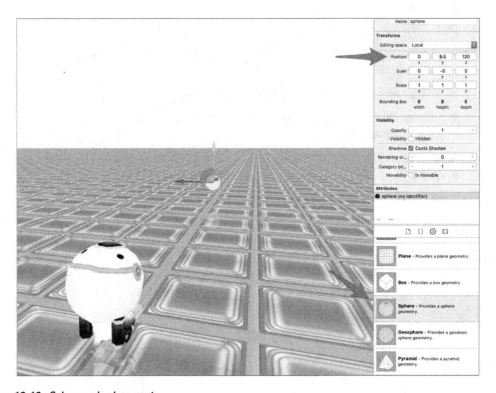

*Figure 16-10.* Sphere node placement

You'll also have to make some size adjustments in the attribute inspector for each of these nodes. Figure 16-11 shows the settings we used for the sphere, but remember that each node will have their own attributes setting based on the type of node chosen.

Sphere

**Dimensions**

| Radius | – | 4 | + |
| Segment count | – | 24 | + |
| Geodesic | ☐ geodesic | | |

**Geometry**

Name  sphere

Identifier  --

Vertices  625

Polygons  1104

**Geometry Morphers**

*Figure 16-11.  Sphere Attributes Inspector*

Now would be a good time to look at several different nodes and their attributes. You have some nodes placed around your screen, which should look like Figure 16-12. Here we've set out three different nodes around the screen. Don't forget to make the adjustments in the node inspector, material inspector, and attributes inspector.

*Figure 16-12.  Multiple nodes*

# Summary

This chapter is just a taste of the power in the SceneKit Editor. Everything you did programmatically can be done for the most part in the Editor. Because this book is just for beginners to get their feet wet, we will conclude here. You should continue to experiment with the Editor and see how your subtle changes can impact your game.

# Index

# Get the eBook for only $5!

Why limit yourself?

With most of our titles available in both PDF and ePUB format, you can access your content wherever and however you wish—on your PC, phone, tablet, or reader.

Since you've purchased this print book, we are happy to offer you the eBook for just $5.

To learn more, go to http://www.apress.com/companion or contact support@apress.com.

# Apress®